"Go South"
Union Organising in the 21st Century
Nigel Flanagan
Edited by Marine Picard

First Published in 2024 by Manifesto Press

MANIFESTO PRESS CO-OPERATIVE |
Decolonising the labour movement series

Manifesto Press
Ruskin House
23 Coombe Road
Croydon CR0 1BD

TYPESET IN *FRANKLIN GOTHIC URW* AND *PLANTIN MT PRO*
DESIGNED AND ILLUSTRATED BY **CORATA GROUP**

ISBN 978-1-907464-63-8

The moral rights of the author have been asserted

studio@manifestopress.coop
manifestopress.coop

GO SOUTH

UNION ORGANISING IN THE 21ST CENTURY

Nigel Flanagan
Edited by Marine Picard

To Jean Flanagan, my Mum, with love.

CONTENTS

PUBLISHER'S FOREWORD

MANY OF US READ and enjoyed the 'bruising' nature of Flanagan's first book 'Our Trade Unions – What Comes Next After 2022?' and the debunking of so much organising theory and practice. That the unions are in a much better place now than they were before the strike waves of 22/23 is obvious but how they exploit that is still up for grabs.

Britain's trade union movement is is oldest in the world, among the most experienced and has dealt with an employing class that itself is the most experienced and, on the basis of super profits extracted form centuries of colonial domination, slavery and imperialist war is both immensely wealthy and determined to retain both power and riches.

Thus, when Nigel Flanagan, author of the provocative Our Trade Unions – What Comes Next After 2022? returns to the common and divergent experiences of the global trade union movement he sets out his premise that British trade unions can usefully look to the Global South for insights and examples of how to organise in the era of increasingly moribund 21st century capitalism.

Of necessity this discussion will continue and Manifesto Press, in partnership with Praxis Press, is committed to publish extensively around the theoretical, ideological and practical problems of the working class movement.

This book is offered as a contribution to that discussion not in the sense that all the arguments are closed off and that this represents a final word but more as a stimulus to continued investigation, the exchange of experiences and the formulation of a common approach that strengthens – in the insight of Karl Marx: 'Now and then the workers are victorious, but only for a time. The real fruit of their battles lies, not in the immediate result, but in the ever expanding union of the workers. This union is helped on by the improved means of communication that are created by modern industry, and that place the workers of different localities in contact with one another.'

His assertion that our unions are in a much better place now than they were before the strike waves of 2022 and 2023 is the foundation of his argument as is his suggestion that this potential is yet unrealised.

This latest book continues the discussion with the proposition that there is so much we can learn from the Global South, about the role of activists and the connection between wider political issues around gender, race, disability and of course poverty and exploitation. The Indian General Strike is a case in point. No doubt that a General Strike in the USA or Germany would attract far more comment, scrutiny and analysis than the Indian campaign.

This book challenges us to look at organising in the Global South but without the blinkers of euro centric thinking. Workers that fight and win in India and Africa have much to teach us. As part of the Manifesto Press 'Decolonising the unions' Project Flanagan has set out the challenge to Go South.

— Nick Wright, 2024

INTRODUCTION

I **N OCTOBER 1945** in an outlying area of Manchester, at a site that is both unremarkable and uninspiring, an extraordinary conference took place. There is one simple red plaque to mark it, but otherwise it is hardly celebrated in British Labour History. In the city where Engels and Marx studied the early developments of capitalism, where the Peterloo Massacre is commemorated annually, where the trade union movement – in a painful childbirth via the Industrial Revolution – was fought for and built by working-class men and women, there is little reference to this 1945 conference. This is a city that was at the heart of the Chartists and the early Suffragette movement. It is not surprising that this city and its great labour leaders and fighters are justifiably proud of what their noisy and violent history means to the working-class movement.

It is regrettable that this conference, the Fifth Pan-African Congress of October 1945, is so little-known or recognised in the UK. Decisions were taken in the Chorlton-on-Medlock Town Hall that led to the independence of African countries – it was a major event of the twentieth century. The people at this Congress included some of the subsequently most famous Africans on the planet. Amongst them was Kwame Nkrumah, who from a British prison in the city of Accra led the people of Ghana to independence. There was Jomo Kenyatta, who in alliance with the Kenyan trade unions brought down the British colonial power and won independence. The great American Civil Rights leader and the writer and Communist Party member WEB Du Bois was there. Many activists and delegates came from all parts of the British colonies to meet and declare their intention to fight colonialism together and seek inspiration from each other. They came from Africa and the Caribbean and met with British-based black activists. Within two decades these black activists had liberated a continent.

Fast forward some 75 years and in a separate part of the world the largest general strike ever held in history is taking place. This time it is India, involving 245 million workers and organised around national demands against the right-wing government of nationalists and free-market capitalists. The strikes are called and organised in the face of some of the most restrictive trade union legislation in the world, effectively making many of the strikes unlawful. Despite police violence and tear gas used against the protests in New Delhi, the alliance of workers and farmers take to the streets in all the major cities of India. This is a truly unique event.

It seems that there is a huge source of inspiration and knowledge in the history of struggles in the Global South that has yet to find its way into the UK movement, despite the unique and central place that the British state has in the history of the world. Workers across the Global South - in many Latin American states, in Indonesia and other former 'tiger economies', in South Korea, all across Africa and in the many former colonised parts of the world - have all fought bravely against colonialism. They have taken on Western multinational companies in large-scale struggles. We need to study and learn from those.

Only ten percent of the world's workers are trade union-organised. In contrast, 40% of the world's workers are either slaves, illegal immigrants or children. In this ocean of exploitation and the ruination of lives, the future of trade unions is vital if it is to be reversed. At the heart of this future are trade unions in the UK. Successful and powerful trade unions in the largest economies of the world are undoubtedly a necessity for the international working class. Without the power and strength of organised workers in the most advanced capitalist economies then the movement is weaker and less able to exert itself over the global power of multinationals and governments. The solidarity and unity of international movements must be enhanced by strong unions in the strongest economies – a global collectivism of workers is an essential aspiration. Without it the global trade union movement is reduced to sectionalism of a national character. It is worth posing the question about why the Indian General Strike has not reverberated more across the global movement Most major global trade unions – ITUC, IndustriAll, ITF, UNI Global – reported the strikes on their websites and sent messages of solidarity. But it perhaps reflects the weakness of the current global unions that this was simply an exercise in expressing solidarity rather than organising it. Most of these global union federations are relics from the 'cold war' global unions set up to rival the Communist International Unions. The Global South by and large has little influence in global union federations who are mostly organised, located and funded by Western trade unions.

Right across the global economy war has now risen once again as a major factor. The manufacture and sales of arms has rocketed upwards on the back of the Ukraine war, the genocide in Gaza and the new cold war with China. The British arms manufacturer (BAE Systems) has recorded a 24% increase in profits in the last 6 months. The US Government has just agreed a military aid package of $61 billion for Israel, Ukraine and Taiwan. The diversion of huge amounts of funding from economic and humanitarian aid is a major trade union issue, that so far has not resulted in any kind of organised trade union response in the UK, Europe or the USA. On the contrary many unions have kept quiet as their members work in these industries. This is a luxury not afforded to many Global South trade unions.

As we have seen in Iraq, military action is swiftly followed by the takeover of economies by global multinationals and western governments. A bonanza of reconstruction contracts and outsourcing takes place, with private western companies employing millions of workers, accompanied by severe oppression of trade unions. Workers struggle to organise in Iraq, and also in Iran, Saudi Arabia, Qatar and across the middle east; their human rights are massively denied.

This sheer misery and exploitation can only be resisted by a powerful global movement. In the UK, where there exists no mainstream political alternative to war and genocide, it is often union members who are at the heart of the national and local campaign against it. 'Free Palestine!' is the slogan of the masses and not of the politicians. Trade Union Leaders like Mick Lynch (RMT), Jo Grady (UCU), Dave Ward (CWU), Daniel Kebede (NEU) and Fran Heathcote (PCS) have all spoken at the national demonstrations in line with the policy of their unions. But not all trade union leaders in the UK speak out against the war crimes of Israel. The General Secretaries of Unite and GMB have made much less strong statements about the call to end arms sales to Israel, acknowledging that their membership amongst the arms manufacturers is problematic for them.

Yet the national demonstrations of hundreds of thousands every week since October 2023 show that workers in the UK oppose the Government and the Labour Party policy on Gaza. Opinion polls consistently show that the public overwhelmingly back and immediate ceasefire. But there is no Parliamentary or Media support for it.

The British trade union movement is currently enjoying a raised and much more sympathetic profile. In *Our Trade Unions* (published by Manifesto Press 2023) we set out to challenge the sudden and popular idea that 'the trade unions are back' in the UK. It was described as 'a bruising read'. We set out to use two examples in Kenya and Morocco to offer an alternative to the community-organising guru notions that came to the UK from the USA. We also looked at the level of rank-and-file power that had existed in trade unions before the defeat of the National Union of Mineworkers in 1984/85. In the 1960s and the 1970s British trade unions were at their most powerful, with over 13 million members and a level of status, influence and a national position that meant they had a veto on government and employer policies. The unions were run from the shop floor, with members exerting control over strike calls and deals. The unions were also untroubled by laws restricting their activities. The closed shop arrangements and secondary picketing were all legal and unions used them on a regular basis to defeat employers. They most famously took on the Tory Government in 1974 when the Prime Minister Edward Heath posed the question 'who runs the country' after national strikes, a 3-day working week and power cuts. The voters threw out the government.

All this was broadly swept away by the anti-trade union laws of the Thatcher Government in 1980 and 1982. The laws introduced a ban on secondary picketing, an end to closed shops (where workers had to join the recognised union at their workplace), full postal ballots for elections and for strike votes, notices required for employers of any strike action and regular postal elections of union leaders.

These laws were not defied by trade unions. They preferred a position of 'new realism' whereby the unions mainly tried to cooperate with the laws, consequently the shop floor power of stewards and workers went into massive decline.

There was a point when the laws could have been defeated, during the 1984/85 Miners' Strike. The miners completely defied the laws, but were defeated mainly because of the power of the state fully deployed against them (Police, Law, Media and even the Labour Party leadership). In response, the unions failed to mobilise in support of the Miners.

The unions declined from that moment on, with membership currently at about 6.5 million. That trajectory is still downwards, despite the recent successes.

The first response outlined even as early as 1980 by Len Murray the General Secretary of the Trade Unions Congress was to change unions into 'servicing' organisations. This meant an emphasis on discount deals for union members on mortgages, insurance and credit cards. It did not halt the decline. This localised service provider model then became reflected in the myriad of European Union initiatives. These notions of 'partnerships' and 'social contracts' were reflected in Directives from the EU designed to enhance legal protections for workers. Progressive Directives on workers' part-time rights, on equality issues and on transfers of workers from one company to another were lauded as the future. It seemed that the future of workers' rights was no longer organising issues but legal ones. But these arrangements, based on a Nordic model of social democrat trade unionism and progressive employers made no difference to workers faced with EU-led austerity measures from 2010.

Nor did the guru methods of organising, manifested in the creation of academies and the employment of more organisers:

they did not reverse 40 years of trade union decline. Trade unions became attracted to the ideas of US organising and even entered into quasi partnerships with US Unions. In effect this one-dimensional internationalism (only working with US unions) did not change the graph for any of the trade unions involved, nor did it in German unions like IG Bau and ver.di; both of whom eventually kept it at arm's length. The creation of organising academies and new organising posts has not significantly changed the trade union density in the UK. Neither did it in other English-speaking countries like Australia, Canada or New Zealand. We broadly think that it is still the case.

But we must reassess the state of the unions now that we are further away from the events of 2022/23. We need to look more closely at the alternatives to guru organising that British unions could use. There are many inspiring examples from the Global South and we need to look at them.

The unions are still not 'back'. But they are in some ways in a much better place to recover from where they were in January 2022. The numbers are still not good, and the recovery is very uneven – but the atmosphere and the context has changed. It is no longer a given that workers in the gig economy or the private sector are too difficult to organise. We used to ask, 'who will organise the disorganised?' – but now we can see that they can and do organise themselves. It is no longer the case that the legal restrictions on unions in the UK makes national action virtually impossible to organise.– The unions have now positioned themselves to resist the Tory Government's 'Minimum Service Levels' legislation by breaking the law.

Perhaps the most promising event has come from a group of workers in Coventry. It is coincidentally the birthplace of the great global union leader Tom Mann, and also the place where a young trade union official called Jack Jones started to organise factory workers through rank-and-file power. In Coventry the Amazon workers, members of the GMB, have possibly broken through the most powerful anti-trade union company in the world. We will look at this extremely important event, where the GMB members have won the right to have a workplace ballot for trade union recognition. The resistance to this from the company has been overcome by the workers.

In January 2022 the unions appeared apparently powerlessness to reverse the P&O Ferries decision to sack 800 workers. The workers were sacked and offered their jobs back on 'zero hours' contracts with reduced rates. It seemed that the familiar pattern was once again happening and that the employers would get away with it.

In early 2023 however we saw the announced closure of Port Talbot Steelworks and the potential loss of 1,600 jobs. It doesn't seem so hopeless as it did for the P&O workers. Their trade union Unite has balloted them for strike action to fight the closures and the workers have voted for it. This time it would seem that the fight is on.

Maybe things are better than they were in 2022. But they won't be if we keep doing the same things that we were doing from the late 1980s until 2021. Servicing strategies and guru strategies did not deliver the strike successes in 2022/23 – members did it. Some unions have done better than others, some have done worse than they claim. So far there are no big national winners. Many of the successes, but not all, appear to be in already high-density workplaces.

This book is arranged in six chapters.

Chapter 1 looks at what the situation is for the UK unions in 2024, their challenges, and some local and national actions and outcomes.

Chapter 2 discusses the national general strikes in India in 2019/20, and the example of a union exclusively for women, the Self Employed Women's Association.

Chapter 3 explores the strategy of 'spiderwebbing' for union organising, describing examples of actions/ organisation by security guards in Namibia and Ghana, and the Orange workers in Madagascar.

Chapter 4 discusses the challenge of gaining and retaining union members, and describes five 'patterns' of organising, inspired by successful smaller or local disputes.

Chapter 5 discusses actions organised in the UK in solidarity with Palestine, and how this can inspire unions. It looks at the role played by trade unions in the fight against Apartheid in South Africa, and how Islam can positively help union organising.

Chapter 6 examines the obstacles to 'rank and file' power in trade unionism, such as the UK Employment Laws and the disappearance of politics inside union workplaces.

As Marxists we analyse our society, we look for signs of change, we dig deep and go wide. In this book we want to present the signs that the working class could be on the move. After all, we have nothing to lose but our chains – in the UK and across the world.

— Nigel Flanagan, March 2024

Chapter 1
The state of the unions

THERE WAS NOTHING QUITE as enjoyable as watching Mick Lynch, the General Secretary of RMT, explaining to a Sky TV News reporter what a picket line was. In March 2023 they tried to use an interview with him as an opportunity to talk up lurid fantasies of picket line violence and intimidation. He wiped the floor with them and was cheered on by many working people all over the country. Quite apart from anything else, he was able to contrast the utter chaos on railways in the UK on days when there was no strike action, and he was able to argue for a coordinated and publicly-owned railway system that delivered reliable services. He went on to expose the unacceptable levels of profit made by privately-owned railway operators.

It was revealing on so many levels, but for our purposes it showed what national action had done for the unions. Mick Lynch also never failed to mention the other workers on strike – such as nurses, teachers and postal workers – who also deserved a better pay deal.

The trade unions in 2024 are in a better place than they were in 2021 before the upsurge in actions. But the underlying problems still remain.

Media commentators have tried to present the post-Brexit, post-Covid-19 and 'cost of living' crisis UK labour market in 2024 as determined by systematic staff shortages and high turnover. They claim some workers are more selective, more demanding, and less loyal to employers, especially if they feel neglected. They choose new work-life balance arrangements. This phenomenon is being studied and named the 'great resignation', the great reshuffle, or 'quiet quitting'. Those problems are common to most Western countries but here in the UK they were exacerbated by a hostile approach by employers. A particular group of workers affected by these emerging factors were the young – over 26% of jobs lost in the pandemic were those of workers under the age of 24.

Yet far more characteristic of the labour market in 2023 was the leap in the number of days lost to strike action – an estimated 3.95 million according to the Department of Employment. Although that does not compare to over 40 million days lost in

1979, it is a huge shift from an average of 200,000 days lost per year in the years from 1999 up to 2021.

In the last year of recorded statistics (2022) the unions lost approximately 200,000 members – the first downturn in 3 years. Of these, 129,000 were estimated to be women in the private sector. These losses seem to be in the private social care and hospitality sectors. So, whilst some unions continue to claim upward surges in recruitment in the last two years, these increases are possibly wiped out by resignations, redundancies and retirements. The figures reported by trade unions in their annual returns do not yet show a marked increase in members or density. That may change and we hope it can be sustained.

Unite – an organising tour de force?

Unite has claimed that it is recruiting about 10,000 new members a month, that it has organised over 1,000 disputes in the last two years, involving over 200,000 members and that over £450 million has been won for workers. These are impressive figures compared to other trade unions and to other years. We are yet to see if this has significantly improved overall membership figures, bearing in mind that Unite has lost 811,000 members since 2007. By looking through the wins recorded on the union website it is however possible to suggest a number of trends.

- In the last year 2023/24 over 100 local disputes are recorded as wins in the private sector. These are mainly in public transports services, defence-related industries, airport services and some manufacturing areas where labour shortages may have positively affected pay award negotiations.

- There are some impressive pay rises ranging from 10 to 38%.

- In 2023/24 the union has recorded 21 local successes in

directly employed public sector disputes, in the NHS and
Council services.

■ There is no clear evidence of success in the so-called
greenfield sites or in the economic sectors where union
density is low, suggesting that Unite is delivering for members
in existing and union-organised workplaces but not in a big
way in many previously non-unionised workplaces.

This more nuanced examination of Unite successes – because
they are successes – helps us to understand what might be taking
place in the labour market. Where unions are already organised
and where there are skill shortages in that particular market, then
unions will do a lot better than in previous environments.

Unite has recently promoted itself as a new style of union, with
an emphasis in winning industrial disputes as a priority above all
else. It was an attempt to distinguish Unite as a different union.
The style was unmistakeably going to be US-inspired, looking
to borrow from the reputation of the Teamsters and the Service
Employees International Union (SEIU) in the USA. It has led to
a change at the top. The General Secretary refusing to attend the
Labour Party conference was a crowd pleaser for ultra-left groups
and was not well-received by the old guard. It was slightly out of
lane for a General Secretary and has recently been compounded
by a reluctance to speak out against the genocide in Gaza.

But the real essence of the change of pace in Unite was to be
its organising strategy, its prioritising of members disputes and
the need to, if necessary, go 'full in' on employers. This is a union
that has lost 811,000 members since its creation out of a merger
of the TGWU and Amicus in 2007. Inspired by the US union
SEIU, they seek to emulate its reputation as an organiser-based
union. In copying the SEIU intensive training in organising
steps and escalating actions, they hoped that they would achieve
breakthroughs in the same sectors – low paid, precarious, service-
type work – that SEIU had shown a way forward on.

It is interesting to note that the SEIU, seeking to differentiate itself from AFL-CIO unions at first through prioritising organising, shifted its priorities in the Obama years to investing heavily in his Presidential election campaigns. They put pressure on him to deliver both workers' rights and his 'Obama Care' health provisions. It has shifted back, out of necessity, towards organising again. Its membership levels have stalled and are currently about 2 million, as it was over 15 years ago. This must have impacted upon Unite's organising strategy as they have sought to publicly demand more from the Labour Party in terms of commitment to workers' rights and jobs.

What is also plainly true though is that Unite has focused mainly on local disputes, involving anything from a few hundred to a few thousand members at most. It has been very successful in the great majority of these. But its aim of building national sector committees and reshaping bargaining back towards national deals has not proved fruitful so far. There have been no Unite national ballots resulting in national strike action either against a single employer, never mind in a sector. Unite reviving its membership levels and bargaining power is at best unproven.

GMB and Amazon

It is this pattern of activity in organising that we might see across all the unions. GMB union has recorded some similar successes, albeit on a smaller scale, again mostly in previously organised workplaces where there are labour shortages. These have mainly been in Ambulance Services across the country, in Asda, British Gas and in some local authority services. Some impressive pay agreements have been reached and GMB, like Unite, has done well for its existing members.

GMB has of course been at the centre of possibly the most important trade union dispute in the UK. This dispute has been years in preparation and falls right outside the comfort zone of any trade union in the UK – the fight for union recognition in the global giant Amazon.

Any analysis of trade union activity in the UK should now focus on what is happening at Amazon and why it matters. The achievement of the GMB members is very impressive. The GMB has successfully won the right to have a statutory workplace ballot on trade union recognition. This has taken a lot of organising activity and the union is confident of winning it. This will be the first time Amazon has had to recognise a trade union in the UK.

Amazon has been subjected to a 'site at a time' strategy set out by the GMB in the UK. Amazon currently employs around 70,000 workers in the UK along supply and delivery chains and directly into 'fulfilment centres' - which are essentially depots. The UK is the largest market in Europe. Its Global Operations contain a hard layer of active anti-trade union management. Its business model of 'click and buy' is the contemporaneous model for gig economies across the world. The American company owned by Jeff Bezos is the world's largest e-commerce company. In 2022 it recorded worldwide sales of $400 billion and a surplus of over $25 billion. Its turnover is higher than the GDP of all but 34 of 213 states in the world – just less than Denmark and just above Egypt.

On a day-to-day basis union activity is very difficult. Work is tightly controlled and supervised, with very little opportunity to gather workers together and talk to them. Union organisers cannot get on site and activists are continually faced with the threat of redundancy or hours reductions, because of the nature of zero-hours contracts and hostile management layers. This is the same pattern all over the world – in Europe, North America, Mexico and many other areas of the world where Amazon is operating. In the UK a significant portion of the workforce are workers with English as a second language, which creates an additional obstacle for GMB Organisers and union activists who are not multilingual.

The temporary and precarious nature of work at Amazon is also massively governed by seasonal workers. It is estimated that Amazon will take on an extra 16,000 workers around the Christmas and New Year holiday periods. This will provide opportunities but also create problems for activists trying to establish a union presence in such a turbulent workforce. But it has been done before.

Given the severe and restrictive nature of UK employment law and the constant blocks and delays contained in them, it is impressive that the Amazon workers in the UK have made significant progress. From early depot entrance-style rallies and some off-site community meetings, the GMB Organisers have linked up with activists and proceeded diligently in traditional union-organising tactics. They established a base of membership, created a significant union presence, applied public and gate entrance pressure and created an atmosphere where the union was a much-discussed issue. This 'atmosphere' was months, if not years in the making and eschewed high-profile leverage tactics in favour of the use of the union hinterland and a focus on building membership.

It was no surprise then when in late 2023 and early 2024 GMB were able to organise a strike ballot win and very disruptive days of action over a pay and recognition claim. Wages are very much at a basic level in Amazon but not the worst in this sector: from April 2024 they were paying a starter wage of between £12.30 and £13 per hour. Obviously a lot of this is due to the requirement to pay Minimum Wage rates and the impact of the labour shortage, but Amazon elsewhere in the world often responds to union militancy by imposing new wage rates without meeting the union. This has been a particular tactic in Europe where national laws require Amazon to at least have a consultative relationship with trade unions.

As noted above the Central Arbitration Committee (a government civil service body with powers to impose a workplace ballot for recognition) has ruled that a statutory ballot for GMB recognition must take place. If Coventry becomes officially recognised, then this is a global breakthrough of real significance. What GMB does with this success is important. They have demonstrated that Amazon can be taken on and pushed back and that their organising strategy in Coventry has worked. But can they replicate it across the rest of Amazon? Amazon will counter-attack and their behaviour in the US shows they would not rule out closing Coventry down. There is no suggestion of that at the moment, but this is a ruthless anti-trade union global company.

GMB has now established a union presence at two Amazon

sites in the UK – Coventry and Birmingham. They have won strike ballots on both sites over pay and union recognition and are pursuing the company through official recognition procedures. This is a significant achievement and should be applauded by the movement. What is pertinent for the movement though is that this has not come up as part of the 2022 cost of living strike wave, but has also been a developing pattern of ups and downs, mistakes made, flexibility demonstrated and solid steps forward. Amazon sought to 'dilute' a workplace ballot on union recognition at the Coventry plant by suddenly recruiting thousands of workers who would be eligible to take part in the ballot. It is clearly a sign that the company know that their workforce is getting union-organised. This is a classic 'greenfield' dispute where a union tries to organise a union where there are no or few union members.

So, what is missing from this strategy?

Amazon believe that they can contain and defeat this campaign. It has not spread beyond Coventry yet and the union appears to either lack the resources or the willingness to quickly and significantly do that. Amazon closed down the nearby Rugeley Centre when they realised it was becoming union-organised. They claim that out of the 2,000 workers employed at the Birmingham plant, only 19 voted for a strike, and that less than 100 took part. They are using their standard union-resistance tactics, centred around messages like:

'We want to speak with you. A union wants to speak for you.'

'The union wants you to pay £14.37 every month for them to speak for you. We believe having a voice shouldn't cost you anything.'

'You don't have to join a union to have your voice heard. We've got you.'

These statements are standard examples of the soft resistance Amazon organises against unions. It is a mixture of aggressive and decisive actions such as closing plants or disrupting ballots, whilst at the same time appearing to be a worker's friend, a partner or a confidant.

To effectively resist these efforts, a union must be strong on the ground and in the workplace. This can only be achieved by an activist presence that is confident and in charge of its campaign. Portraying the union as some kind of 'outside force' or a 'third party' can only be countered by workers being the drivers of the campaign and being the people with whom the company has to deal with.

There is evidence that the GMB has two possible fault lines in this campaign. The first is that there appears to be very little workforce-based leadership. Understandably at the early stages of a campaign, when the union is the minority, it is the union officials and organisers who front the campaign. But nearly two years into the campaign there is no developed collective shop floor leadership. This is a common problem – where union organisers lead and then move on, after which the union flattens and sometimes reverts back to its previous levels. Organising to avoid this is a crucial part of the strategy a union needs to adopt. There is a temptation for unions to move on after the headlines, leaving very little behind them. Hence the much quoted 'Labour of Sisyphus' story of unions doing the same task forever – like the Greek myth requiring him to roll a boulder up a hill and rolling it down again as a punishment for fooling the Gods.

This may also be behind the absence of a strategic plan to spread the action as quickly as possible. There are at least 14 other plants to be organised. There is a giant Amazon plant virtually in the heart of Manchester at Trafford, surrounded by unions, offices, Labour Councils, MPs and a huge population. This is what we refer to as a big 'union hinterland'. It is the use of this hinterland that may be crucial to winning. Many Labour Councils and local Health Authorities use Amazon extensively to order for example office supplies or other equipment, as do schools, colleges and universities. A truly National Organising Campaign would bring all these elements together with other trade unions to support or threaten a boycott for example.

The lack of sufficient resources within GMB to take on Amazon nationally might be encouraging them to think they can win as long as they hold the ground in the West Midlands. Coventry should be talking to Trafford and other places. There is no doubt that GMB Organisers have thought about this but somehow it is not manifesting itself in any activity.

There are possibly resource reasons for this. The Amazon campaign does appear to be happening in only one region of the GMB – the West Midlands. Activating it in other regions does seem to be the next step. The GMB is a union in internal turmoil at the moment. It is outside the mainstream of the movement in relation to the issue of arms manufacturing spending, has an internal scandal apparently unresolved from the last leadership and, like all unions, would rather be having a partnership relationship with Amazon like it does with companies like G4S. This contradiction between the local energy and activity in Coventry and the seemingly unhurried position of the national union is definitely a problem.

Bluntly the local activists are the best advocates for workers of spreading the strategy and the actions, but they need the resources of the union. This mismatch of needs and resources may contribute to a successful containment of the dispute. Unleashing the rank and file is not simply a romantic delusion. It is a strategic necessity that the lay side and the bureaucracy are as one on this. Amazon has not yet resorted to the levels of aggression and belligerence in the UK that is has exhibited in the USA. The UK remains Amazon's largest market in Europe, and it is unlikely that they will try to 'live with' the GMB.

National Organising Strategies

If the GMB is not financially or organisationally up to the national campaign against Amazon, then why not bring unions to work together on this?

Sharon Graham won her election campaign as General Secretary of Unite partly on her promise to fight Amazon. She and her team targeted it, quite rightly, as the obvious test for the union movement in the UK and was quoted saying that Unite was the union to do it. Of course this has not happened.

It would be a good thing if Unite and GMB combined to unionise Amazon. It would be a huge blow to Amazon. The unions could divide the plants between them, agree a joint strategy, set up a joint national union committee and make national bargaining a key demand. If possible, they could talk to RMT about organising some of the Amazon supply chain workers. They could talk to CWU about organising some of the delivery workers. This is the kind of strategic organising thinking that is lacking. Of course, Amazon UK will resist national bargaining and of course they will indulge in all the paraphernalia of North American union-busting tactics. They do that stuff everywhere. But – here is the example from our history – organising the dock workers and the mass of unskilled workers into so-called 'new unions' in the early twentieth century was not deemed possible until it was done. This example – from the years immediately before the First World War – is instructive. Dock workers were the most precariously employed in the UK. They turned up every morning to a gate or pen. A supervisor would look over them and pick out the men he wanted. Often this was a case of picking relatives, mates and those who had offered bribes. In some places it was also done based on sectarian religion. Every day the dockers did not know if they were going to get work from the supervisor. On top of which if they were no ships to unload nobody got paid.

It took mass action to organise them, in strikes such as the Liverpool Transport strike of 1911, organised by the great union leader Tom Mann. The organising strategy was to spread quickly from dock to dock, in a nationally-coordinated plan.

Activists in the union movement must raise these sorts of strategic organising questions. It is not enough that unions run organising techniques training courses that are mostly centred around questions of recruitment (though it is very important). We need to rethink our entire organising strategy and not just our local techniques. In a shrinking movement with fewer and fewer resources we must forget turf wars and inter-union rivalry. We should instead pool our efforts into 'de-badging' campaigns and having a union movement trying to move forward on *shared* organising strategies, rather than being in competition.

We can see possibilities for this in public services. There is no doubt that UNISON, GMB and Unite are in competition in national local government and the NHS. They raid each other's memberships; they hold separate consultative arrangements and are often left with contradictory positions in front of the employers. UNISON has yet to reach the 50% threshold required in its national ballots – astonishing for a union with such resources and an active lay side. GMB often accepts deals and Unite seems to take longer to consult. These are broad-brush assumptions, but the combined effect is that the negotiators are handicapped by a lack of member mobilisation, often because of separate approaches.

Someone has to say - 'this is not working' and do something about it. It is essentially an organising question, yet these arrangements and outcomes continue year after year. Again, it is the lack of any real shop floor input that seems to allow the continuation. It should not be beyond the wit of the three unions to combine to campaign for a national pay deal, with a collective consultation and recommendation. It should be organised around a strategy for national claims attached to a national recruitment campaign. Contrasting this with the organisational ability of Indian Trade Unions (see Chapter Two) or the Kenyan Security Guards (see *Our Trade Unions*) is a painful exercise, but it needs to be done.

There is plenty of evidence to show what RMT, ASLEF and TSSA did achieve with simultaneous and rolling coordinated action in the same sector. Why is it beyond the capacity of NEU and NASUWT to achieve the same?

Unlike most other union movements, the UK has a unique arrangement in that there is only one National Confederation for the trade unions – the Trades Union Congress (TUC). The TUC is quite widely considered to be pretty ineffectual on some of these national questions, neither able nor willing to try to organise the unions into coordinated actions. The response to the question of a general strike in 2023 over the cost-of-living crisis saw no meaningful response from the TUC. Once a number of unions appeared to rule it out, then it got no further.

Yet unions have been robust enough over the Tory government's 'Minimum Service Level Agreements' to the point of saying – we will not abide by them. One General Secretary even went as far as to say that if he was a worker who get notice to be at work under the law, then he would definitely be feeling sick that day! Unions have put some effort into getting employers to agree that they will not use the Act in the public sector.

National Organising is the question. It is a matter of fact that the two previous 'strategies' of servicing and organising gurus have not delivered increased membership. To quote Lenin from *What is to be Done?*

> 'We need not fear mistakes. What we should fear is persistence in a mistake, refusal to admit and correct a mistake out of a false sense of shame.'

We have to push back on the idea that firstly everything is going really well, and secondly that there is nothing to be learned from looking at and criticising what has been done in the new wave of strikes.

Trade unions need to develop a shop floor movement that will properly develop its strength and take advantage of the energy raised in the recent strikes. But they are still looking to organising gurus and North American strategies, still reverting to servicing and to leverage tactics rather than developing the strongest weapon it ever had – mass membership built by a shop floor movement. Worse still – the organising strategies of the successful unions in the Global South are not being used to revive the union strength in the West. That revival would be a great boost to trade unions all over the world. India and Africa are showing us the way forward.

There is currently a wave of analysis and discussion taking place around the events of 2022 and 2023 in the UK trade union world. It is worth reminding ourselves what these were and to take note of the noticeable differences in local and national disputes, both in actions and outcomes.

Signpost for future UK union organising

The first and most obvious new development was the fact that national and local strike ballots were being won across the movement and across the country, despite the myriad of legal obstacles and the lack of recent experience of such actions. This is significant. There have hardly been any national disputes of significance involving successful national ballots since the early 2000s. There was no battle-hardened base of union activists, by which we mean those union activists who have previous experience and knowledge of organising and winning big strikes. Nor was there a significant or deliberate deployment of organising resources at the start of 2022. What followed was won by mostly new activists and by union staff who were probably surprised at the balloting outcomes. One broad feature of the successful national ballots (in CWU, RMT, NEU, BMA, RCN, UCU) is that these were won in public sector services, albeit in some cases delivered through outsourced organisations. These are areas where union density was already higher compared to the rest of the economy, but none where the density compared to the peak of union density lost since 1979. In effect union membership in many parts of these sectors is often below 50% and there is no evidence yet that industrial action has produced a significant surge in membership. CWU remains strong in the Royal Mail but in many other parts is still an organisation that represents the minority of workers. RMT itself acknowledges that its density outside the core areas of the Rail Service is poor and could be much better in many areas of ancillary work, such as cleaning. RCN in the NHS is in essence a minority union, albeit a substantial one.

There were a number of national ballot failures. UNISON only achieved a 30% turnout in its ballot of Local Government workers and again in its ballot of NHS workers in England. NASUWT also did not achieve the 50% threshold target in its national ballot. Despite winning previous national ballots, UCU also failed to achieve a 50% turnout in its last ballot and so lost the mandate so hard fought for in previous ballots.

In contrast there were hundreds of ballots and disputes in smaller localised employers, with high turnouts and sustained periods of industrial action. It is clearly easier for unions to win local ballots than national ones. In local disputes resources are targeted much more easily and communications to members is far easier to organise and achieve than across a national membership with a small or dormant activist base. These local ballots were in both the private and public sectors and were characterised by being mostly in already union-organised areas. With close deployment of union organisers and a focus on union activity directly with members, this intensity of organisers and resources was not possible in national disputes.

Another key feature of these groups of workers was that they often deferred to local officials in terms of leadership and representation, as so much of the dispute is in the hands of officials via the power invested in them by the anti-trade union laws. Again, a level of worker supervision by unions emerges in these disputes, with much of the conduct of the dispute seemingly miles away from locally elected representatives. Comparing the UNISON NHS wide ballot which was lost under the 50% threshold with the high turnout and very popular activity by the Wirral Healthcare Workers is instructive. They were both organised by the same union. Looking at the many ballots and disputes run by Unite in the private sector is also interesting. They were won in areas with an already decent union membership, but a lack of activists. They were also characterised by a generous deployment of organisers, and ballots won with very high support for strikes on a very high turnout. They often involved significant strike action that was well supported by local networks and solidarity activities.

The UK union members have created a chance for the unions to revive. Let us move on to where that revival might find inspiration – away from Europe and North America.

Chapter 2
'Baharat Bandh!' The General Strike in India and actions in the Global South

I N 2019 AND 2020 a number of national general strikes organised by a coalition of trade unions, farmers organisations, students and street workers caused unprecedented national disruption in India. Called by ten of the major trade union organisations in the country and supported by 1200 trade unions, it brought over 245 million workers out on strike. It was massively unreported all over the world and yet it is the largest ever general strike in history.

It was scandalously off the front pages of newspapers and barely reported on TV news in the UK, at a time when the government was cuddling up very closely with India's right-wing government and talking of new trade deals. That the UK, with its Indian communities and its role in the history of colonialism, should not deem it worthy of reportage and commentary is unfortunately typical of its journalist intelligence. What is more disappointing is that in most cases there is little coverage and analysis of the labour movement. It is puzzling that we have not descended on Indian comrades, looking for learning and inspiration. The scale of the protest organised in the most difficult of conditions surely demanded that we seek to understand, if not emulate, exactly how this was done.

Had these events taken place in the USA or in Germany we would no doubt have been able to access many reports and analyses of the events. The fact that we have not yet done that leaves us seemingly insular and unable to move out of a Western colonial mindset, as if we have nothing to learn from the Global South and the former colonies. The notion of the 'mother country' is in the psyche of the British Union movement. Seen in a global context, the strike waves of 2022/23 in the UK do not reach the levels of significance of the Indian General Strikes. There has to be a wider outreach of solidarity, unity and collectivism than simply what happens in the West.

Whole areas of India were shut down, railway lines were blocked, and there were riots and confrontations with police in most major cities. The alliance of workers, farmers, informal workers and students was a major achievement against a government intent on making the poor pay more, privatising vast parts of the economy, stirring up hatreds that had been used by colonial Britain and exercising a foreign policy allying itself openly with the USA and Israel over Gaza, and against China and Pakistan.

Perhaps the most obvious reason for the under-reporting is that the protests were partly successful, with the government of Modi backing down on its proposals over agriculture. Within months the Modi government withdrew its proposals to tear up controls over prices and corporate takeovers that had triggered the strikes. This was a clear and emphatic win for the strikers, and in particular for the farmers.

Approximately 66% of India's workforce derives its income from agriculture, which contributes to 18% of India's GDP. The three anti-farmer bills undermined the minimum support price buying schemes of the government, and put 85 percent of the farmers who own less than 2 hectares of land at the mercy of monopoly wholesalers, with obvious consequences for the farmers and workers.

The context for trade unions is significant. There are nearly 500 million workers in India. 85% of them work in the so-called informal sector – agriculture and farming, street vending and related operations. The economy has a huge number of workers in the private sector, industry and public services – over 75 million in total. They are organised into a vast number of trade unions (1200, which is a problem in terms of organising) in 13 different Confederations. They are mostly loosely allied to the Congress Party, the Communist Parties and the various Left groups. They are based on sectors and geography. Density is very difficult to calculate as many unions operate on a one-off payment joining fee, irregular subscriptions or charge nothing at all. Verification of membership only occurs every ten years and was last done in 2021. The ILO has calculated that there are about 14.5 million union members belonging to the 13 National Central Trade Union Organisations. There are very restrictive anti-trade union laws in place, making it difficult to recruit and represent workers, and the International Trade Union Confederation (ITUC) has reported in its Global Human Rights Index that the situation is getting worse, with strikes banned in many parts of the public sector.

The Signposts in the strike

There are a number of very important elements to the Indian General Strike that need to be amplified.

Firstly, it is the scale of the strikes. It has been estimated that 245 million people have taken part in the strikes, representing a quarter of all adults in the country. In contrast, the ruling Bharatiya Janata Party (BJP) under Modi received 229 million votes in the last election before May 2024. That the movement could create an active protest involving more workers than the numbers who voted for the Government is incredible. To compare this to the UK if 14 million people voted Tory then the unions would need to deliver a General Strike of 16 million people! The only union federation not to support the protests was the pro-BJP Bharatiya Mazdoor Sangh, which has allegedly lost support as a result. Amongst the rest there was a broad range of organisations, including most strongly the Union Federations supported by most Left parties, including the big Communist movement and the Congress Party.

Secondly it required significant organisational strength to deliver the strike. The sheer diversity of sectors and organisations involved, the heavy human rights and labour law legislation in place, the geography and distances involved and the overtly hostile political climate – including the media – presented big challenges. Indian trade unions are typically under-resourced, informal, splintered across sectors and lacking in most of the facilities that exist in the West. They rely almost entirely on lists, networks, mass meetings and local organisation rather than having a national machine they can mobilise. There are very few organisers or full-timers even amongst the national leaderships, and much of what resource they are able to use comes from whichever Central Trade Union Organisation they belong to. In the context of an almost completely informal farming sector, this was a big organisational challenge.

Thirdly the demands were national claims. There was no attempt to use local grievances as a trigger for a dispute – all the messages were about general problems cutting directly across the politics of the government. The claims were anti-nationalist, pro-worker and

anti-poverty, and they were about privatisation and subsistence.
The joint trade union charter of demands was:

I   Direct cash transfer of Rs 7,500 (US $101) to all
         families who earn less than the income tax threshold.

II   10 kg free ration per person every month to all in need.

III   Expansion of the Mahatma Gandhi National Rural
         Employment Guarantee Act to provide employment
         from the current 100 days to 200 days work in rural
         areas with enhanced wages, and extension of this
         programme to urban areas.

IV   Withdrawal of all anti-worker labour code changes
         and anti-farmer laws.

V   Stop the privatisation of public sector corporations,
         including those in the finance sector. Stop the
         corporatisation of government-run manufacturing and
         services entities in railways, ordinance manufacturing,
         ports and similar areas.

VI   Withdraw the draconian circular of forced premature
         retirement of government and public sector employees.

VII   Provide a pension to all, restore earlier pension scheme.

Mobilisation around these and the farmers' demands overlapped
and complimented each other. The support of trade unions for
the demands of the rural poor was not a given. It was the role of
activists in Left parties and in trade unions to bring them together
and make the solidarity and coordination needed happen. The
opposition was fierce. The police were deployed in numbers to
break up protests, Hindu nationalist groups were deployed to
disrupt picket lines and the media went into an overt pro-Modi

campaign. The Government even intensified the demolition of mosques, a move designed to whip up Hindu extremists and to intimidate Muslims. This represented a distinct challenge for activists – both in relation to Muslim and to Hindu workers.

Which leads to a fourth element of the strikes. They were generalised into support for other social issues on the demonstrations. There were slogans and speeches proclaiming opposition to Modi's 'Citizen Amendment Act' designed to deny Indian Muslims their rights as asylum seekers. Indian Trade unions demanded that Modi ended an agreement with Israel to replace 110,000 Palestinian workers with Indians looking for work. There were parallels with the anti-Bolsonaro movement in Brazil, which eventually led to the re-election of President Lula. The politics of Modi were seen as the same as Trump's – narrow, nationalistic, corrupt and anti-Muslim. There are many state governments within India that are run by Communists, Socialists and Social Democrat parties. These mostly supported the protests, and this too contributed to the strength and breadth of the opposition. With elections due to be held in May 2024, these developments are to be welcomed.

A national organising strategy was clearly used, the strikes achieving mass support with minimum resources and with a significant number of actors in the trade union core and the hinterland. It involved many trade unions around the same platform, with Parliamentary speakers from those supporting political parties and a heavy emphasis on the turnout of members and their own networks.

The Self Employed Women's Association India – SEWA

There is one union organisation that stands out as an example of those demographic areas that the unions in the West and in India have so far not been able to organise. It was full square in support of the strikes and was an active part of the protests.

94% of women workers in India work in the so-called 'informal sector'. There are many social, economic and structural reasons for this, but the outcome is that women are often overwhelmingly working without contracts, insurance, or legal protections, on the streets or at home, harassed by the police and subject to sexual violence or threats. They are uniformly on low incomes and are subject to all manners of economic, social and physical pressure.

The organisation was formed in 1972 as an offshoot of the Textile Labour Association, the largest Indian textile trade union. It emerged in the city of Ahmedabad and spread initially across the state of Gujarat. It currently has 2.9 million members – compared to 33 million in the Indian National Trade Union Congress, a combined total of 27.1 million in four Communist confederations and 17.10 in the pro-BJP trade union BMS. It is one of the fastest growing trade unions in India. Ideologically it is formed around ideas from Gandhi and has the following basic principles enshrined in its constitution:

- *Satya* (truth).

- *Ahimsa* (non-violence).

- *Sarvadharma* (all faiths, all people).

- *Khadi* (economic self-reliance).

Its role in the strikes was partly down to its social location between organised formal workers and its own membership, with family members often overlapping the two. SEWA has sought to organise its membership to take an active part in the protests. These are the most vulnerable of workers, so the consequences of the Modi programme are not difficult to imagine. In addition, if the demands of the trade unions are successful, that can only assist the position of these women workers. SEWA is affiliated to the ITUC and takes an active part in its functions.

The organisation is not within its critics but there is no equivalent in most of the West. It has its own Cooperative Bank which specialises in microloans for its members – a point of contention for many, as the microloan and microcredit system is often associated with exploitation in many very poor parts of the world – and much emphasis on self-empowerment and development. But there was in this strike a national effort to mobilise its members out onto the streets. It is the economic circumstances of its membership that makes it unique. After all, there are many women in other trade unions, but not many unions try to organise these workers. In an economy like India's, that is a weakness. It challenges the idea that unions cannot organise the self-employed and the precarious, and there is much to be learnt from its successes. As well as promoting its members issues with politicians and with other trade unions, it mobilises to protest.

What next for the Indian Trade Unions?

The ultimate test for the General Strikes will be the Indian General Election, held between April and May 2024 – with the result announced in June. There are 968 million voters and there is an assumption that BJP and Modi will win a third term. As a result of which there will be further deepening poverty, more anti-Muslim actions and increased cooperation with the USA and Israel.

This will manifest itself in the economy with continued neoliberal policies that will put millions at risk of increased poverty. India's economy is the fifth largest in the world, but with levels of poverty still unimaginable in the UK. The challenge to the trade unions is that overcoming the right-wing nationalist government requires more than they have delivered so far. There are too many trade unions in India and too many Trade Union confederations. The economy is being rapidly reshaped under their feet, to their dire disadvantage.

But on the back of their recent strikes, they can be confident that the resistance is there and that their strategy of national mobilisations has strong support. Whatever is the outcome of the General Election, the Indian Trade Unions have drawn a line in the sand for the working class all over the world.

Chapter 3
Spiderwebbing tales!

I **N OUR LAST BOOK** *Our Trade Unions* we set out the organising style that has become known as 'spiderwebbing'. In it you can read about the Kenyan Security Guards or the Moroccan Call Centre workers. This tactic, or style, or approach – call it what you will – is based on the notion that union will only grow if ordinary members take part in activity. Rather than rely on officers of the union or employed organisers, we go straight to members. Rather than rely on burnt out activists, we instead go directly to the members with a straightforward task – take ten names from us and persuade them to join the union. If they are already a member, come to the meeting and ask each of their ten names to take another ten names from us.

It needs organising and preparation, but it works. There is no 'leader identification' training, no 'constructive conversation' training, no 'escalating actions' planning as beloved of the gurus of organising. There is mapping, lists and volunteers with a briefing on a few bullet points.

There are many examples, but we have chosen a handful here to give a more varied flavour of how it operates. These are all real examples from various parts of the world, and we have named certain organisers to allow a more personalised story. After all, organising is really and mostly about our own stories, about sharing our examples and passing them on.

The term 'spiderwebbing' came from Moroccan activists who related it to the story of the spider making a web over the entrance to the cave in which the Prophet was hiding. The meaning being that even though the web may be flimsy it will be sufficient to hide the entrance and protect the Prophet.

Namibia – Security Guards

Namibia is a country blessed with great natural beauty, an abundance of mineral resources and a relatively stable system of government. Previously it was under German colonial, then it was annexed to Apartheid South Africa. It had a particularly brutal experience of colonialism. The German occupiers carried out a genocide of the Herero and Nama tribes; after which the South Africans maintained a system of white brutality and violence.

Namibia is rich in diamonds, gold, silver, coal, copper and uranium, and has a labour force of just over one million, the bulk of whom work in the informal and agricultural sector. The largest trade union federation is the National Union of Namibian Workers which is closely affiliated with the SWAPO Government. SWAPO – the South West Africa People's Organisation – was previously the armed wing of the anti-apartheid resistance. Fighting alongside Cuban troops in the 1970s and 1980s, they were partly responsible for the military defeat of the white South African army. Now the government has embraced free-market forces and has retained Western mining companies with undertakings that there will be no nationalisation programmes. China is also by now the second largest trader with Namibia after South Africa, and is involved in a number of infrastructure projects in the country.

Elsie is a young single parent who has been temporarily deployed as a union organiser by the National Association of Transport and Allied Workers Union. Along with her colleague Kavaka – also a young organiser – they had been tasked with recruitment of Security guards in Namibia. The guards were mostly employed by G4S and covered some of the most important parts of the small Namibian economy – airports, mines, banks, embassies and hospitals. They also guard shopping malls and some factories.

They had no formal background in trade union work but were both energetic and intelligent. The union had funds from a global trade union to use on an organising project. Working with the only other two full-timers in the union – the General Secretary and his assistant – they completed a mapping exercise of where they wanted to build the union, starting on G4S contracts. G4S in Namibia was essentially an apartheid-looking set-up – white managers and Black security guards. Management was very hostile and even straightforward recognition of the union was not agreed. There was no way in via management. They had tried walking from one site to another, but it was lengthy, tiring and often a bit of a depressing experience.

They needed a new plan and a new approach.

This time they set about going round the workplaces not to recruit as such – although they always asked people to join – but to come to a meeting about the union and see how it would work. A time was agreed, a venue booked, some materials sorted out and a short presentation organised on how they were going to unionise G4S and what it would mean. About 20 people turned up, mostly women. The presentation was basically – these are the places nearby where we need to sign people up – are you willing to help us? Here's a list, here's a union t-shirt for you, and these are our claims to G4S. Some transport was organised and dates to carry out the actions were agreed. It was to meet up every day for a week and a quick debrief.

Namibia 2017, Organising in the gold mines in the Namibia desert. This is the transport union organiser Kavake. Many of the mines have very tight security around them but with cooperation of the Miners Union Kavaka was able to get in and sign up the Security Guards.

Within a week they had recruited 500 plus members. Not all the 20 turned up to help from the initial meeting, about 12 of them did, plus the two organisers. 500 in the context of a union whose national membership was 6,000 – mainly railway and airport workers – was quite a big deal. This was new income to the union and gave them credibility arguing with G4S for recognition. This led to other activities – such as attendance at the morning guard 'parades' where the workers were addressed by management before being dropped off at their guard site. The 'spiders' would turn up with leaflets about the union and further meetings.

They had also identified what the issues were that the workforce wanted to be dealt with. It wasn't a question of having no idea – after all the spiders are security guards too. But even within such an obviously hard job like security work, some problems are more urgent than others. Workers complained of many things, but mostly:

■ Very low pay, out of all proportion to what we discovered that companies were being charged for a Guard compared to what a Guard received. The slogan 'Guarding Wealth, Living in poverty' as used in Kenya was also used here.

■ No breaks and no facilities, many guards were in place for up to 12 hours a day, often with no shade, no toilet facilities and no opportunity to get regular refreshments.

■ Unofficial punishments for not being in place if a supervisor calls, sometimes being dropped off out of town and left to walk home for miles.

■ Nepotism amongst the workforce where favours and easier placements are given out to relatives of supervisors.

■ Lack of safety from extreme violence against guards who were ill-equipped to respond – no radios, no uniform, often just a stick and a whistle in some cases.

Namibia 2014. The first small team of Namibian activists who started their two year organising campaign in 2014. The organiser Elsie is on the right on the phone. In their first week this team signed up 500 new members in Windhoek, the capital of Namibia

Both Elsie and Kavaka's wages were funded by a solidarity group from Finland called SASK, a workers-rights organisation funded by Finnish trade unions. When they heard about what was happening, they sent a small delegation out to meet Elsie and Kavaka. All were amazed and more funding was offered to further the project.

The next stage was the mines. Every mine is well away from any population centre as such. Namibia is vast and only has a national population of about 2.5 million people. The mines therefore have extensive barrack arrangements for miners and for other staff, including security guards. In cooperation with the National Union of Namibian Mineworkers, Elsie and Kavaka set off across the Namib desert and many miles of open roads to start recruitment at mines of the security staff. This was again a big success, with guards joining and contacts being made to create a spiderweb of mining contacts across the country. This was further developed at the port of Walvis Bay – a very important hub port for trade to southern Africa from the Atlantic.

The power of these organised workers should not be confused with the small numbers relative to the UK or India. The Walvis Bay port is a major facility and serves exports and imports from the whole of Southern Africa, including Namibia, South Africa, Zambia, Zimbabwe, Angola and even across the Kenya, Tanzania, Uganda, Rwanda and parts of Congo. The security guard service if completely unionised has significant power, which is why the Transport Union (NATAU) wanted to unionise the Guards.

Enough income was forthcoming to deploy two more organisers from the ranks of the new members – Helga and Kapuchea. They too set about the same task – call meetings, ask for volunteers, brief them, build a web and then take the numbers back to the union and the companies for bargaining purposes. Since then, all these organisers have moved on from their temporary work with the union and left behind a real legacy of success and increased union power.

Ghana Security Guards

Ghana is, like Namibia, one of the most comparatively stable countries in Africa. Being the first to win its independence from Britain in 1957 and having undergone a successive series of coups and changes in government, it emerged in the 1990s with a series of democratic elections that had passed peacefully and with a growing economy. Despite the debt crisis it suffered in the late 1990s, it is managing to grow and prosper in some economic sectors, particularly in new technologies. Its main sources of income are gold (the world's largest producer, overtaking South Africa) and cocoa production (second only to Côte d'Ivoire), and its biggest trading partner is Switzerland (cocoa and gold again). It has a population of about 30 million and a workforce of 12 million. It also suffers from a large informal agricultural sector (over half the national workforce) in which there are 2.7 million child workers.

Within this context the trade unions have two rival confederations – the Ghanaian TUC and Ghanaian Federation of Labour. In broad terms the TUC is mostly public sector and is the oldest organisation, having thrived and withered under various governments (having been an important part of the Independence struggle), whilst the GFL is a new self-styled independent trade union organisation.

The Security Workers Union in Ghana, affiliated to the GFL, was run by three full-time staff, a General Secretary Mensah and his two assistants. They operated mainly through legal challenges and some recognition deals allowing them to bargain, the main employers being Ghanaian but also including the ever-present G4S. G4S operates a kind of 'franchise' system throughout Africa, allowing local companies to use their name, logo and reputation without expecting them to follow any international standards or policies. Any complaints to London HQ of G4S would often be met with a shrug.

The challenge for this union was to grow in the capital, Accra, but also to establish a foothold in the important port of Tema further down the coast. Security guards in a place like Tema could have great power if fully organised.

To assist the union in this it was arranged for its first session that Elsie would come from Namibia to assist with preparation and presentations, along with a G4S worker from Finland who was a union activist. There were also representatives from the solidarity organisations who were funding the work. The issues for the workers were as above for the Namibian Security Guards – low pay, informality of employment, breaks, bullying and harassment.

Extensive mapping had been carried out and the union pulled in a meeting of about 30 members. Amongst them were a number of experienced activists and the whole group was split into teams with maps and lists and sent out across Accra. In one week; they had 1,003 new members, adding to the 4,000 they already had. The same cheap resources – t-shirts, caps, lists, transport and expenses – were used to achieve this and it was then fed back into the union lists to assist in bargaining meetings.

A particular area of hitherto unknown problems was a number of luxury car showrooms. Guards on less than $2 a day would be guarding dozens of vehicles worth $100,000 or more. At night these cars were often the subject of attempted theft or vandalism. The lowly-paid guard was expected to deal with this. It was in this kind of situation that many guards were injured, assaulted and in some cases, killed. Absence from work through injuries did not usually allow for sick pay arrangements but would be tied up in complicated insurance claims.

As in Namibia the biggest test for the union is sustainability, and this depends mainly on keeping the spiderwebs going. This is difficult when the sector has such a high turnover, and workers are always looking to move on to better opportunities. Chiefly it has to be part of the union strategy for long-term development. They must negotiate after their rush of membership. They need better facilities, a proper recognition agreement and discernible outcomes from campaigns. Without these it is just a recruitment drive – and any union can do those.

The exercise was repeated in Tema, the major Ghanaian port, but with less success. This reflected the lack of preparation and the lack of local contacts before the first approaches. Consequently, a lack of knowledge of the employers, the working conditions and the absence of a local base made it appear as though this was just an attempt to make money. 'Unions only eat your money' was a common response.

The Ghanaian security Workers Union did not go from strength to strength but collapsed internally for reasons beyond its organising drive. In many ways tensions were caused by growing too quickly and overwhelming the small lay leadership. Income tended to drag behind recruitment so that many new members did not immediately bring in new income but did bring new pressures on the union. Collection of union dues was not easy from employers that had no offices and no bank account. But these problems have been overcome in different parts of Africa and there is no reason why Ghana would continue to be an exception to this. Significantly, since then however other general trade unions have taken up the challenge and many of the guards have been transferred to new unions.

Madagascar and the Orange Workers

Madagascar is the fourth largest island in the world, with a population of just over 30 million and a workforce of 13.4 million. It is a very poor country, with poverty affecting nearly 92% of the population and 69% living on less than one US dollar a day. It has a large child labour problem, with 8% of urban children and 22% of rural children employed in manual labour including mines. It produces 80% of the world's vanilla and its economy is largely dependent on fishing, tourism and agriculture.

Trade union density is difficult to establish and the system of industrial relations is an inheritance of the French Colonial system, but without the guarantees of works councils being organised by employers. Recruitment of individual workers is the route to bargaining power.

One of the few employers in Madagascar to at least pay lip service to trade union rights is the giant French company Orange. They employ about 800 people in Madagascar and have a recognised union that was all but abandoned by the workforce as it was unable to bargain improvements from the company. There were approximately 200 members in the union. 400 of the 800 workers were based in an Orange HQ building in the capital Antananarivo, with the rest dispersed amongst some shop-front operations and maintenance. These were clearly some of the better-paid jobs on the island and the workforce was mostly young and well-educated. These were the jobs that a lot of people wanted and nobody who had them wanted to lose.

The leader amongst the workers was a young woman called Holy, who at the time of the campaign was seven months pregnant. There were many issues that the workers were upset about but there was no clear idea about how to even start. The obvious problem was the low membership and then the refusal of management to take

the union seriously, despite Orange in France signing a Global
Agreement to recognise trade unions around the world. It was
them signing this that had led to a very successful campaign to
unionise Orange in Africa, led by UNI Global Union. Madagascar
wasn't expected to be a worthwhile or fruitful effort though.

Holy and her colleagues got a group of enthusiastic members
together to meet. They talked about how bad things were and how
they were ignored and came up with various tried-and-tested ways
of encouraging workers to join, but were very pessimistic. They
had tried to call a 'big meeting' for all workers after work in the
hope of getting some along, hoping that the novelty of an outside
person from UNI Global Union would interest them. Instead, it
was planned to book a room for two lunchtimes inside the HQ

Ghana 2016. One of he teams of 'spider web' workplace activists operating in Accra in the capital of
Ghana in 2016. On their first week they signed up 1,000 new members. With them is Peter Jorgensen
the President of the Danish Union Forbundnet who funded much of the activists expenses.

and invite workers to come and meet the union and sign up. To
facilitate this, they bought oranges and drew smiley faces on them
with a little invitation and turned up at the entrance to the HQ
early in the morning. As most of the workers arrived from out of

town on a company bus at a regular time, it was easy to stop and invite them all personally and give them an orange. The volunteers then welcomed workers and took them to a table to talk to various spiders who had lists and details to check people off and talk to them about problems at work. As a result, over two lunchtimes they doubled their membership from 200 to about 400.

None of this requires much training or resource, just the understanding that asking people to help out in simple and obvious ways is often the quickest way to build up numbers. It does require preparation and a bit of cheek. It also requires follow up in that the union activists must take the new branch or union forward. If that bit is not done it just leaves a legacy of disappointment.

From the beginning the Orange workers were very committed to planning and agreeing their own strategy. They did their mapping – which was straightforward. They had little information on existing union members, so part of their strategy to engage one-to-one was also to find out who were already union members. They set out their room with cabaret-style tables, two spiders at each table, and as people arrived they were shown to a table by other spiders who acted as greeters. Immediately after each session had finished they sat down and updated the lists and analysed who they had signed up and from where. There was also a discussion about feedback.

The entire emphasis was on Holy and her team running and organising this process. They did not have organisers working with them or trainers accompanying them and trying to assess their activities. What they did get was briefings and suggestions from union officials who were only there for a week. They won recognition and became active members of a global Orange workers campaign.

Being part of a larger campaign made a lot of sense to them. This was an important element in encouraging other workers to join up – that it was part of a national or African or global plan. It is this factor that is often underestimated in local organising campaigns: that workers, rather than being praised by union organisers for being 'exceptional' in a geographical or demographic sense, are part of a wider cause or campaign than just themselves. This is a crucial part of any long-term organising plan for a union – where does it take us?

Workers of the world unite!

Some of the various global union federations in the world are not as independent of ideology and influence as they might wish to appear. There are constant conspiracy theories (which have a ring of truth to them) about the funding of mostly US trade union solidarity organisations, offering money to trade unions as part of a continued cold war against the International Left. The most spectacular example ever of this was the successful effort to wrestle control of Solidarnosc in Poland and turn it into a Catholic and pro-Western institution, whose purpose was gone when the Communist Government collapsed. Solidarnosc is now predictably a tiny shell of an organisation, with policies that continue to be further to the right of most Polish voters. In Hong Kong, the so-called independent trade unions served only to promote the 'yellow umbrella' movement and were conspicuous in their use of US flags and placards calling on Trump to save them. Recent scandals inside the ITUC suggest that corruption and related politics are not – nor ever were they – a Global South problem.

The promotion of trade unionism is however not to be contained if politics and justice go hand in hand. In recent years trade unions have been a driving force in defeating Bolsonaro in Brazil with mass demonstrations and voter drives, in India as we have discussed and also in countries like South Korea, Indonesia and Malaysia. We must learn about these struggles and encourage workers to know about them.

We have termed this the de-colonisation of the trade unions, which is to remove the remaining colonial mind set of Western trade unions. Only by embracing the lessons of the workers of the world, and not just Europe and North America, can we inject new enthusiasm and inspiration into our ailing UK movement. Don't applaud the Indian workers – copy them!

Madagascar 2018. the French multinational Orange Telecomms workers are out catching the morning shift. The leading activist is Holy, sat on the wall.

Chapter 4
The organising of disputes and patterns of organising

LSEWHERE WE HAVE ESTABLISHED that the unions position is precarious in certain parts of the economy. In IT, Banking, Hospitality, Retail and low-paid gig work – the union density is often in single figures nationally, and completely non-existent in some companies. The union density that used to exist in manufacturing and in nationalised industries has gone and with it, millions of members. In most cases the union institution has remained behind but manages to survive often via mergers or by rebranding themselves. We need look no further than Unite, which is now 811,000 members smaller than the combined strength of the two unions that merged in 2007 – the once mighty TGWU and Amicus.

But it would be a mistake to see the downward curve as the death knell. There are 'patterns' of organising that are beginning to emerge in the hundreds of smaller or local disputes that can point the way forward. There is huge potential in what has been achieved by the various Health Care Assistants disputes in the NHS organised by UNISON. There are many public sector and private sector victories organised by Unite and by the GMB – including Amazon – that are also revealing a new energy in grassroots organising. Several patterns have been identified from the actions taken by those workers.

Firstly, if you were a low-paid, gig or platform worker – what would prevent you from joining a trade union? Here are some statements from precarious workers:

■ 'We don't know what a trade union does, how it works or how it's supposed to help us.' This is very often the case with young workers, there is a generation gap in terms of knowing what trade unions actually do. Most young people will never have come across trade unions at work or in education.

■ 'They are not concerned with our work, it's the work of others mostly in schools, the hospitals and the Council.' This spreads across generations of workers. It's the idea that only if you work in the public sector will unions be able to help you. There are exceptions – the railway network and the postal services – but even there the outsourced non-core elements tend over time to become non union-organised.

■ ''It's dead money, subscriptions are too much and we're still not clear what we get for it.' Particularly from the lowest paid in the most precarious jobs and sometimes most often amongst immigrant workers. UNISON and other trade unions notice that when workers do not have union 'deductions at source' (when union subs are taken directly from your wages and passed on to the union) then direct debits for unions are amongst those that get cancelled in cost-cutting actions by low-paid workers.

■ 'The boss will not like it and says we don't need it.' All workers experience this, an example is the way in which Deliveroo managers tried to get delivery outlet owners to report delivery workers who were participating in strike and protest actions. Or just take as another example anything that Amazon do.

In the context of working conditions, these objections are real. Joining the mainstream trade unions on low wages still seems like paying with no obvious gains for the worker. What do they often get – a newsletter? An email? Even a message from some urging them to vote Labour? If workers join and only receive this level of response, then it is hardly surprising that workers leave.

The level of retention amongst trade unions is a real concern because of the above. Union membership has recently been likened to a bath getting filled with both taps open, but no plug in. UNISON often manages to recruit 160,000 new members a year, but then loses approximately the same, so any progress is at best incremental or is wiped out by leavers. This is difficult for unions to change and the servicing strategies of the 1980s and the 1990s have not succeeded in changing it, as discussed elsewhere. There are however some ideas from that era that have persisted.

All unions try 'recruitment weeks' for example. This is when all officers and workplace reps are urged to spend a week recruiting people to the union – an activity that 'spiderwebbing' insists happens all year. With a stall set up in a canteen or a building entrance there is the appearance of activity. Usually, it does not involve much more than that, and it is not massively successful in recruiting at the rate needed to change the national density levels. Recently there has been an interest in so-called 'Call Centre' organising where new members receive a telephone call to welcome them and to try and answer any questions they have. This is a good way to start the relationship with new members when there are not enough workplace representatives to cover the new members. The call centre will also call up people who have just left to ask them why, and to see if they can be persuaded to stay. But unless it is part of a sustainable strategy and plan, it will always seem like token efforts. These are largely futile exercises unless linked to a wider strategy.

It is no surprising therefore that union density in most parts of the economy continues to curve downwards. Despite the big surge of strike actions and national ballots there does not appear to have been a dramatic enough increase in membership. Not all the unions won national ballots even if they had them. UNISON did not reach the 50% turnout threshold in its ballot of Local Government workers, in fact only managed a 37% turnout. NASUWT missed out on a national ballot because it narrowly fell short of the 50% turnout. Both UNISON and NASUWT counts though came with heavy yes votes.

It may be that the outcome of national disputes did not match the expectations of members. Union members voted to accept some national deals that again fell short of the claims submitted, even taking into account that there is an element of 'opening claim' levels before negotiations begin. The average wage settlements in 2023 were 6% at a time when inflation had reached double figures in certain months, and the cost-of-living crisis had led to many urgent and unavoidable financial pressures on workers and families. Some national disputes also involved other issues that were as important to unions (UCU – Pensions, RMT – new terms and conditions) but most were straightforward cost of living. In the absence of an all-round knockout blow win there has been a flattening of mood amongst many of the union strikers from 2022 and 2023. There is still national action going on – with successful ballots in PCS, NEU and BMA, meaning that some unions will carry on the fight, but the scale is less than last year.

Patterns

In the light of the literally hundreds of successful local disputes, where wage rises were frequently better than nationally agreed ones, it is useful to identify patterns to strikes and how they are organised. More so it can give us an indication of how to meet the challenge of sustaining membership levels.

One – Assessment and Preparation

The first pattern tends to be one of confusion and gathering everyone together. Where do we start?

Ideally, we have a national or regional organising plan, that is agreed with lay leaders and is well resourced, and that the targets chosen are done so as part of this plan. By this we mean: is it a target where we have a reasonable expectation of winning? Do we have members there already? Is it a 'hot shop' - a worksite with an outstanding and obvious issue that workers feel strongly about. Is it a strategic choice with importance to the employer, in that winning here will hurt the employer the most? Have we got members or contacts there already? Is there anything going on at the moment that allows for union activity – a meeting or similar? The Healthcare Assistants dispute that recently ended in victory in the Wirral on Merseyside was a good example of all these factors coming together. A brilliantly run campaign, it exemplified much organising good practice.

Conversely it could be something that takes us by surprise. An emergency announcement by the employer over closures or redundancies for example. Or it could be a workplace issue that has prompted action and reaction by workers. At the moment it is more likely to be this.

The most important considerations at this stage are:

I   What's our base? Do we have a critical mass of members or contacts to move to immediate spiderwebbing or do we need to find people?

II   How, where and when are we going to meet the workforce?

III   What are our resources? In addition to our base (as above), what other resources must we have? Organisers are important but do we also have solidarity contacts? Lists of members and contact details? Facilities to assist the workers?

IV   Who are our allies? Who is on our side and what can they do? Who is responsible for contacting who?

V   What are the aims? Either in the context of the strategy or the demands of the members?

This first pattern is one of the need to respond and to gather forces, to assess and analyse. This should always be done with the workforce – but often isn't and here lie the first seeds of later problems with sustainability. The union – and especially the organisers – should not be leading the dispute or deciding its aims. They are there to help plan and to assist the democratic process. Obviously, this involves a steady process of advice and encouragement, but an officer- or organiser-led dispute often ends badly when things get difficult for the members. At this point the officer/organiser can become isolated from the consequences of defeat and as a result, from the members.

Perhaps the best example of this part of the pattern can be seen from the Moroccan Call Centre workers who were faced with Works Council elections in every call centre in the country. The government controls the dates for Works Council elections in every sector and suddenly announced six months' notice for the next ones, held every four years. The union UMT (Union Marocaine du Travail) had a small group of about 150 members and activists in an industry of 50,000 workers. They had to go through a very quick process of selecting which companies they would stand candidates in and where, they had to choose candidates and then they planned a series of actions and agitations to raise support for their candidates. They had no existing places on any Works Council in this sector and therefore had no base other than their group of 150 volunteers. The union moved an organiser from the hospitality sector and sought the assistance of a global organiser from Tunisia – a former General Secretary of a cleaning union

Morocco 2015. These are the Morocco call centre activists who in 2015 won the national works councils elections, winning recognition in 14 different contact centre companies. Morocco is the French language call centre capital of the world.

who had survived a nine-month imprisonment during the Arab Spring of 2011.

Their planning and mapping of resources was done within one week. They decided to contest elections mainly in the city of Casablanca (by far the biggest in Morocco, and location of approximately half of the call centres in the country). They decided to campaign internally, inside the centres not outside, and printed leaflets with candidates' names and photographs to blitz the centres. The candidates would hold little rallies outside the entrances and even produced short films to be passed around on WhatsApp. This quick, swift process is an example to be followed.

They won the elections – see *Our Trade Union* for details.

Second – Opening Moves

The second pattern is one of mobilisations and engagement. What next?

The mobilisation of members is often a necessary part of escalation if the negotiations and bargaining have not gone well or have even been refused by the employer. Although unions have consultation rights (if they are a recognised trade union), most employers will try and sit through this, seeing it as an unavoidable exercise without changing their minds.

Mobilisation may of course mean balloting for industrial action, in which case the lists and the spiderwebbing become essential. Every member on the list should be contacted by another member to remind them to vote (so as to meet the threshold), and to vote with the union recommendation (to strengthen the hand of negotiators). They should ask them if they will help in phoning other members, check their postal details and check they are watching out for the ballot paper in the post (the law does not allow online ballots and replacement ballot papers can be ordered if one hasn't turned up). Finally, they should remind them of the dates and times of any meetings – online or otherwise – where they can talk to other union members and representatives.

This approach always works in local disputes. It also denies management a 'right of reply' as they are not party to the call. Some union activists think that indulging in email or social media wars with managers are the only way to get the message out. The pattern is – the more you talk to members, the more they will support the recommendation and will 'own' the outcome.

It is important to stress that members will most likely have no knowledge of the restrictions, obstructions and frustrations involved in attempting to follow the letter of the law in balloting. The union has to give the employer a seven-day notice and a copy of the question on the ballot paper. It then has to officially notify the employer of the outcome of the ballot, and finally the union has to give at least 14 days' notice of when the action will start, naming specific dates. The union then will have its own national structures to authorise any action and that itself may lead to an unforeseen pause.

It is part of the pattern that at this stage, after successful mobilisations, members become frustrated at the apparent slowness of events. Hence the importance of engagement and communications – most efficiently done by spiderwebbing.

Not all escalations will mean going straight to balloting. There may be a need for public rallies or similar events to get support together and demonstrate the collectivist nature of the dispute and the solidarity of allies – in which case again the lists and the contact details are important. It needs to get everyone as involved as possible. Organising staff and officers of the union should offer support and access to resources but should step back from carrying out the roles of activists. Speakers at rallies should be workers and allies or senior people inside the union who are organising solidarity such as a General Secretary.

One of the best examples of this type of organising was actually amongst UCU members at Chester University, who in 2021 went through a succession of spiderweb exercises from their list of volunteers. They organised a rally in the centre of Chester over the issue of redundancies of ten percent of the teaching staff and were anxious to have a noticeable turnout. Their membership had already increased to just over 350 and out of 80 redundancies announced they had approximately 50 at risk of losing their jobs. Many of the staff live and work a long way from Chester and it was in the middle of the summer holidays (July). Nevertheless, they used the spiderweb techniques to build attendance at the rally, had the UCU General Secretary as the main speaker plus a number of other trade union speakers. They got over 400 at the rally. This fed quickly into a consultative ballot of members or strike action to protect jobs. The success of the rally and the enhanced effort that went into the spiderwebbing led to a decisive yes vote. All down the line the organisation of lists and the spider activities were organised by branch activists, resulting in a vote that empowered the union in negotiations. Although the job losses went ahead, no UCU member was made compulsory redundant, thus meeting one of the early aims of the campaign.

Third - Breakthrough

The third pattern is one that may emerge or not – the actual dispute. At this point, if the organising has been thorough and disciplined then the prosecution of the actual dispute should be easier – though no dispute is easy. There are many tensions and contradictions and there will be fluctuations in mood and emotions. The strikers will start to realise that this pattern of ups and downs will affect them and the members, and will tempt them into mistakes or miscalculations.

It is very important that the members are consulted and involved about the amount and pattern of action that is planned. The balance between minimising the loss of pay with maximising disruption is a delicate one. Trade unions are stuck in their own lazy patterns of action for example, one day, then two days, then three days. Employers like to sit out one-day and two-day strikes. Regular action of three days or more can disrupt a whole week of business. Rolling action by different groups at different times can also be difficult for employers to manage to cover. The fact is there is more to the 'escalating a day at a time' pattern, and there is more to an immediate and indefinite strike. The key to keeping support is to keep asking members to decide based on what they know about disruption and on what they know they can or cannot afford to lose in pay.

Striking is not easy to organise. There are legal issues for the trade union organisation around numbers and the supervision of pickets. There are roles to be organised to make the strike as effective and as well-supported as possible. These roles will include:

■ Lead picket to liaise with the Police with management and with the union officers.

■ A picket supervisor at each picket.

■ A comms or social media person who will publicise the strike in conjunction with the union.

■ A well-organised treasurer who is able to use an account to receive solidarity donations, can deal with any issues of strike pay and generally make sure that finances are considered at every point.

■ A negotiating team of strikers who will attend meetings and report back.

Management will do things designed to make members nervous and afraid to strike. They will sometimes seek to disrupt picketing and provoke reactions by taking photographs, standing next to pickets, calling the Police, or encouraging other workers to come into work. They will also be operating out with the picketing to minimise the impact of the action. Sometimes it's successful. It's important to stress that all organisation of pickets must be done by strikers – they know their people, the significance of different workplaces, and the likely impact of different types of action.

Strikers will become frustrated that nothing has happened, that it appears that management are not going to take any notice of the strike, that the strikers are losing money for nothing. There will be rumours about who is in work and what they are saying. There will be people talking about going back to work and there will be some allegations of bad faith over where the dispute has been led. All these things are perfectly normal and will happen in any dispute. It is not great organising to ignore it, nor is it good to respond to each and every bit of dissent. There are various things that can be done to help with the resolve, to offer reassurance and some confidence but mostly to make sure members feel that they are ultimately in control of what happens in the dispute.

It is important to gather solidarity from allies. This helps to keep the strikers more confident. This means donations to a strike or hardship fund, solidarity visits from other trade unions, speakers from other groups of workers in dispute and the organisation of social and other picket line events to liven up the mood. Without all these things, a strike can become low-key and isolated, and attendance at picket lines will drop off.

Being part of a national network of Broad Left groups who will assist in organising this outside support and also offer some experience is important, but they must be groups based on solidarity and unity. There are some very effective sources of support for strikers which can help with publicity and solidarity. Foremost amongst these is Strike Map UK. They have their own solidarity lists and groups that will publicise the dispute, encourage support for the strike and provide much more awareness amongst trade union activists in the movement who can help. Their badge of honour comes from being named an extremist group by the *Daily Mail* but their actual reputation comes from organising support and solidarity. No strike should take place without Strike Map UK knowing about it.

A further strand of support can come from local Trades Councils. Historically the trades councils have been a serious and active part of the movement in all locations. In the past they have organised protests and meetings for trade unions that have disputes in their local areas. They have delegates to regional TUC meetings and also of course to the annual TUC. They can be another layer of support and should be approached by strikers.

A local social media and press effort is important. We also need to use our own resources to help publicise disputes and activity. In this sense the use of *The Morning Star* as a source of solidarity is equally important. Many trade unions subscribe to it nationally and all unions contribute to its daily output. There is no surer way of attracting national interest inside the movement than by contacting the *Morning Star* – read by so many union activists, leaders, MPs and public figures. They are always looking for news items around the trade union world and so can be very influential in drawing attention to the needs of a particular group on strike.

The creation of a union 'hinterland' from where support can be drawn is really important but not decisive if it is limited to expressions of solidarity. Although the *Morning Star* and Strike Map UK cannot call workers out on strike, their role in the preparation and the construction of the hinterland that can deliver action on the ground is very important. The bits of the hinterland that can deliver are the ones that unions will try and mobilise. These will include:

■ Other trade unions, not just in the UK but around the world. The most recent example was the coordinated action by Amazon trade unions around the world on the so-called 'Black Fridays', where unions joined together over the strikes in Coventry.

■ Politicians in India have joined the General Strikes and used the momentum to create an electoral coalition against Modi and the BJP government.

Fourth - Regrouping

Strikes are not always successful. A big knockout moment rarely happens – although it sometimes does. It used to be more common in the 1960s and 70s when unions were more powerful, but these days all the odds are with the employer. Conversely strikes are rarely a complete failure either, with strikers sacked, the union smashed and the employers completely triumphant. That used to happen especially in the 1980s but not even in the 1984/85 Miners Strike was the union completely broken.

The pattern tends to be something in the middle, sometimes more acceptable to the employer than to the strikers, and vice versa. The dispute may end with an agreement that has been reluctantly accepted or mutually accepted as fair. There are many examples of one dispute just being part of a cycle of conflicts, where employers keep coming back for more. The responsibility usually lies with the employer – it is mostly their actions that prompt a response from the union.

But as a dispute comes to a conclusion there is a real danger that this may precipitate a union decline. There are a number of reasons for this and it is important that our strategy for sustainability sets a pattern for renewal and continuity. There are many workplaces that maintain a reputation for union militancy with high density and there are a number of features to those situations that should be part of a sustainability strategy.

The union must have the back of the activists. Any hint from the union that the activists are a problem may result in victimisation. In the first instance any 'return to work' agreement must include a 'no retribution' clause, especially if there is still a bad industrial relations atmosphere. These return-to-work agreements are often overlooked in the middle of relief and the relaxation at the end of a strike, but they are important to strikers (who may still have little confidence in the 'good faith' of management). Don't let the employer phase out the best activists one by one, be on guard for the comeback further down the line.

The settlement must be exhaustively consulted over. It is unlikely that everyone will be happy. The spiderwebbing here is very important and useful – members like to talk about the settlement, not simply receive it with a ballot paper. They also prefer to see a recommendation from the strike leaders but may also appreciate the honesty of saying 'we can't recommend acceptance or rejection'.

Where possible and appropriate there should be some kind of coming together, in celebration and as a thank you. Creating our own collective memory of the efforts everyone made is very important and will help with sustaining the union life after the dispute.

Fifth - Sustainability

There are two elements to the end of a dispute – managing the flatness and building sustainable strength. As workers return to normal working, depending on the outcome, the workers may begin to feel disengaged from the union. When this does happen it is a real test of leadership. When members are back at work after a dispute it is a return to many things they don't like. They will be supervised again, managed and tied to tasks. Sometimes this manifests itself in disengagement from the union. Membership might fall, attendance at meetings will be smaller and there will be a feeling that management are back in charge. There will be some disillusion and disappointment as management may push back with individual case work or other proposals if they sense any exhaustion or 'conflict fatigue' – both of which are both natural and understandable.

There is a point when the union machine – its organisers and facilities – will also withdraw. This is understandable if the perceived 'emergency' is over and there are other calls on the union resources. There is danger in this moment for the members. It is why officer/organisers have a responsibility at the beginning of the dispute not to be seen as the agitators or substitutes for leadership by the strikers. This is irresponsible at worst and tactically regressive. It lays the seeds for future retreat.

Unfortunately, there have been examples where some organisers become the dispute, and not the strikers. Organisers on social media posting about their own involvement, rather than the strikers' – 'proud to be with them' and such other tweets – is presenting the idea of union troublemakers stirring up the local workforce, and this does impact on the strikers and on the employer. Newspaper interviews with organisers and officers, whilst sometimes necessary to protect strikers who are afraid to speak out in public, can turn into outreach by staff and a distancing of lay leadership from the control of the dispute. It is no secret that one union in particular sought to isolate and control one leading activist, who was developing a public profile and putting a lot of energy into solidarity work, by removing him from a WhatsApp group and calling him to disciplinary meetings. The message to the rest of the strikers was 'We are in charge, not you'. The employer will have noted this and it does not help the activists.

This means that a sustainability strategy has to be built into the plan. From the beginning of the dispute the strikers and the union must have an idea of what a 'win' looks like and how they will live after the – successful or otherwise – dispute.

A sustainability strategy must include:

■ A plan – what will we need and how do we get it?

■ Trained and experienced lay leadership.

■ Written agreements on trade union recognition and a return to work with the employer on facilities and access to new employees.

■ Consistency in union structural involvement – no sudden withdrawal made worse by too high a level of management of dispute by officers from the start.

■ Intensive and constantly updated mapping of workplaces and departments.

■ Resources to back up the plan, including technology, finance and time.

■ Integration and involvement in the wider union structures at national and regional levels.

■   Allies – who else is committed to keeping a strong union? Customers? Allied unions? Communities?

At a local level these are all attainable, and if pursued from the beginning, do become the core of organised union strength. The transition from a dispute into organised power is not easy, given the flatness and the relief that comes after a dispute. But overseeing these elements as part of the formal outcome is a useful way of keeping activists reminded that the union life is an ongoing effort. The credit from a recent success soon runs out.

In 2016/17 shop workers in the city of Ekaterinburg in Russia had agreed their organising plan based on these factors. They were employed by the German supermarket and retail company Metro, had no recognition agreement and little workplace power. They had a small group of activists, and the union had some resources to try and support them, including an organiser. All the sites were mapped, all the activists and the organisers were trained in techniques, tactics and rights, and the union started a recruitment campaign based on spiderwebbing and spreading out from various supermarket sites. They quickly ran into management opposition, with activists targeted with disciplinary threats and isolated from other workers. Despite this, the membership doubled inside the company in Ekaterinburg to give the workforce a near enough 50 % density. However, this was not enough to persuade local management to recognise the union in this company in this city.

Ekaterinburg is the fourth largest city in Russia, many miles to the East of Moscow and beyond the Ural Mountains. But it is a growing commercial centre and for Metro it was an important place for them to establish themselves in the huge Russian market. The importance of this meant that the union could and did through UNI Global Union and the German trade unions put pressure on Metro in Germany. Without the pressure on the ground and the clear organising aims, this would have been a very tough place to recruit new members and sustain membership.

Finally

In all of these patterns the role of the member is the most important, followed by that of the activist. From a cold start a union presence can only be created and sustained with member or shop floor activity. Even where there is an issue that needs resolving (a so called 'hot shop') the development into an organised workplace or company has to be the work of the members and the activists. This is where 'spiderwebbing' has shown itself to be efficient in getting messages to workers and getting them together in meetings to make decisions.

This then requires focus by trade unions, making all other activities secondary to the organising campaigns.

It also requires committed and generous resources, especially at the beginning.

This is why we have termed this effort 'full-spectrum organising'.

Chapter 5
The national campaigns and full-spectrum organising

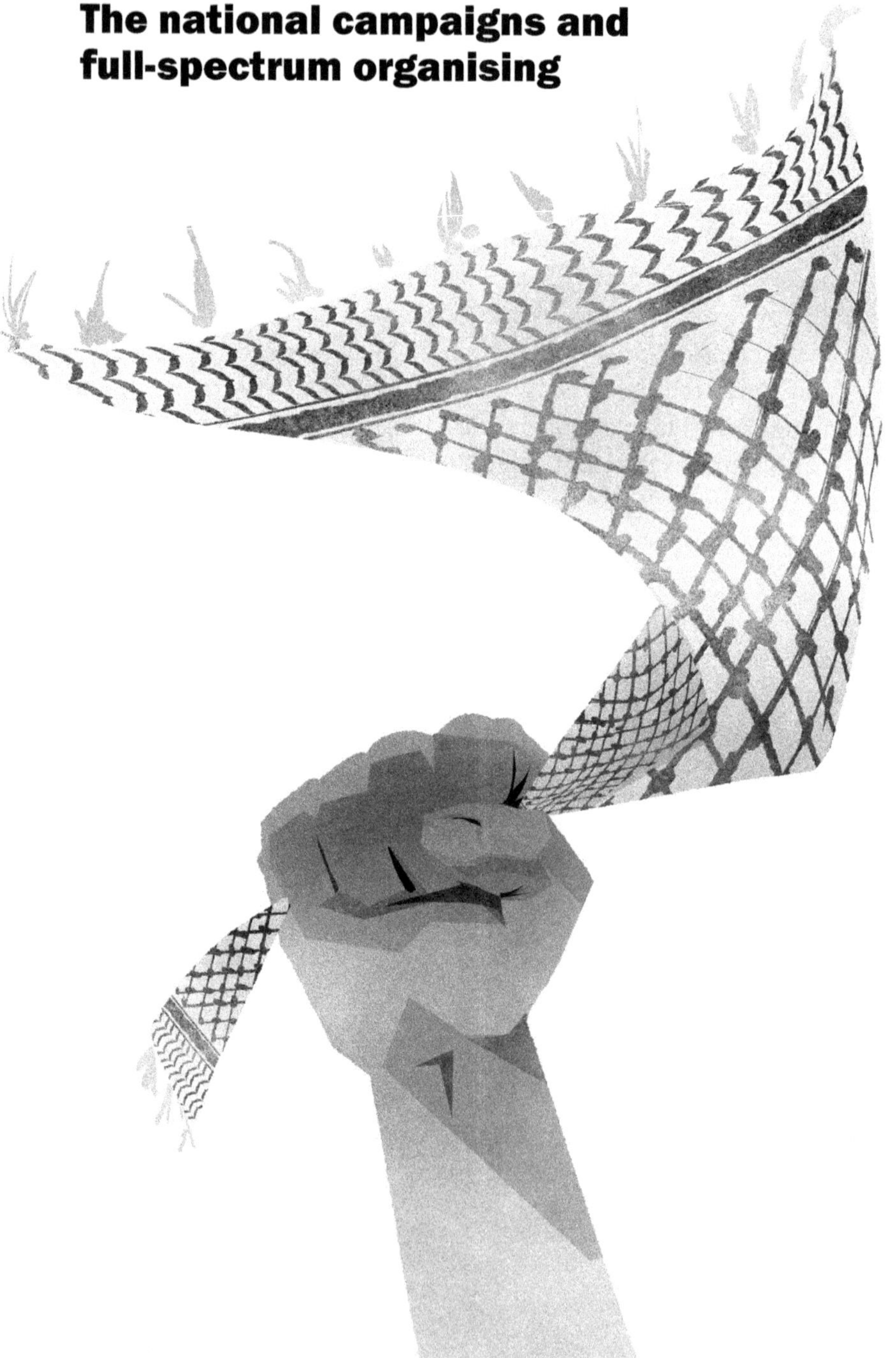

THERE IS CURRENTLY IN THE UK one of the biggest and most persistent mass campaigns ever organised. It involves hundreds of thousands of people on marches, supported by millions of people.

The campaign against the genocide in Gaza and for an immediate ceasefire has mobilised millions of people to turn out and protest over a sustained period, in many different locations. It has brought together an immense coalition of organisations, institutions and communities, both formal and informal, and enjoys no mainstream support either in parliament or in the media. On the contrary both Parliament and the media have led the way in attacking, demonising and undermining the campaign. A plethora of new laws, denunciations, bans, condemnations and even legal actions have failed to prevent the mass opposition.

Prominent amongst the supporters of the campaign are the trade unions – but not all of them and not with equal vigour.

At a national level many trade unions have been from the very beginning affiliated to Stop the War and the Palestinian Solidarity Campaign. The General Secretaries and Presidents of these unions have addressed the rallies and meetings all over the country – in defiance of the many Labour politicians who have refused to support the same cause, preferring instead to side with the organisers of genocide and atrocities. The RMT, UCU, CWU, PCS, NEU and ASLEF have all been proud to have their national leaders at the front of marches and speaking from the platforms.

The mobilisation of support has been even more impressive at the many local levels of the campaign. There have been coaches funded, protests supported, speakers provided and encouraged, lobbies on pension funds and even lobbying of local councils to back the calls for ceasefire. The support for boycotts and the local condemnation of MPs refusing to back the people of Palestine have been growing and are persistent. We do not know the outcome of all this activity but we do know that it has so far pushed politicians away from their initial uncritical support for Israel, that the Government is in crisis over this and other problems, that arms sales to Israel and economic and other boycotts are making it harder and harder for the West to continue to ignore the war crimes and the violence. From a trade union perspective too it has pulled back the curtain on the profound influence of the Israeli Government and its embassy on Labour politicians. The unions that support the campaign have not flinched from putting resources and solidarity into the marches and protests.

From an organising perspective there are a number of interesting features to this campaign that might be helpful to trade unions.

- There is clearly a huge number of young workers attending these campaign events, attracted not just by the support for Palestine but also to the wider issues of ethics and justice. The enemies of trade unions in terms of employers are often the enemies of the Palestinians in terms of their economic and moral support for Israel. Boycotts of the same companies that unions are fighting for decent pay and conditions provide a clear example of overlapping interests and aims.

- The mobilisation of numbers is not a one-off affair. It is not a limited protest. It is evidence that working-class people can be organised in big numbers to support a cause they believe in. There is no huge pot of 'Red Gold' funding this. All resources, even those from unions and communities, are limited and face competing demands, but this issue has led to some phenomenal fundraising – in the middle of a cost-of-living crisis.

- All regions of the UK have had record turnouts and participation, not just once or twice, but on a weekly basis. To have had thirteen national demonstrations in London – the biggest at 800,000 and the smallest at 200,000 – but with people attending from all over the country is also unprecedented.

■ There is a massive amount of self-organisation and coordination taking place within local communities. The resignations of many Labour councillors and the forming of new voting blocs has clearly been prompted by opposition to the Labour support for Israel.

■ Many trade union members and activists are not as conflicted as Labour politicians and some trade union leaders appear to be about the rights and wrongs of the situation in Gaza. There is no equivalent campaign in size or of any meaning in support of Israel. This does suggest that the ethical and moral elements to working-class consciousness have not been swept away by some post-modern rampant form of amoral thinking.

What does this mean for national organising strategies for trade unions?

There is a need for unions to think through what they can learn

Ramallah 2016. The training of Palestinian Bank workers in spider web organising techniques in Ramallah in 2018. The union doubled its membership in a matter of weeks from about 1,000 to 2,000. Its leadership and activists had to overcome the many barriers and injustices of the Israeli Occupation.

and absorb from this movement and its nature, its operations and its meaning. It would be a mistake to think that the spirit and the radicalism of the protests can simply be transferred to the union movement. It is a distinct task to build organised union power that requires more resources and more strategy than organising mass protests. Governments will deploy the Law and the Police, tear gas and even the military against mass protests and will do the same against national trade union action. In response it will requires all the power of the unions and the working class to be used to meet this effectively. It requires therefore a commitment of resources, a move to political strategising and coordination between unions nationally, putting aside turf war tactics and sectionalism.

We see a different pattern of resistance from organised labour in the Global South to that deployed in the West. As we saw in India, the main rallying point was the list of national demands. In Brazil it was to get rid of Bolsonaro – a clear national demand that was delivered in the election. A very important example of a national demand by trade unions that led to successful outcomes was the actions of the trade union movement in Peru in 2023. The far-right coup in December 2022 against President Castillo, a former teachers trade union leader, led to organised strikes and protests demanding elections, culminating in a great 'march for peace' in the capital Lima. Although this was a great democratic crisis the unions mobilised their forces along with the pro-democracy protest movement.

South African Trade Unions and Apartheid

Perhaps the greatest of national union protests in the last 40 years was in South Africa. Faced with the political, economic and social dominance of Apartheid, Black workers and communities employed a number of forms of resistance. There were peaceful protests mainly organised in the 1950s, followed by the African National Congress (ANC) and the armed struggle, the Youth uprisings most famously around the events of the Sharpeville massacre in 1976, and of course the international boycott campaign targeting Western companies and their profits from South Africa. The trade unions have played a central role in the overthrowing of Apartheid. Black workers until 1979 were not allowed to organise in trade unions and there were no Black trade unions. White trade unions were not allowed to take them in as members and in reality, none of them wanted to. But the power of organised Black workers was to offer the most potent challenge to the South African state and its economy.

The first wave of strike action, all of it entirely illegal but carefully organised by activists in factory meetings – where gatherings were still technically possible – led to a first walk out by 2,000 workers at the Coronation brick and Tile Company in Durban January 1973. In what became famous as the Durban strikes, over 100,000 workers were on strike over low wages by March of the same year. It was the biggest challenge to Apartheid Laws since 1948. Tear gas and police were deployed against the strikers but eventually the employers imposed wage rises on the workforce to end the strikes.

The Durban strikes led to massive organising efforts across the economy. Black workers met at work, in factories, mines, docks and in many other workplaces, to form illegal trade unions. The State found it hard to target union leaders as they were spread across so many locations and, being illegal, organised much of their work undercover. Three distinct elements emerged from these activities:

I   A necessary but effective shop-floor union tradition, where unions became organised mainly by local leaders with power based on rank-and-file control. The unions operated many illegal networks to bring workplaces together, across sectors and geographical areas. Unlike many other African trade unions, they were not based on the organising models of European trade unions with their structures and demarcation elements, but on informal networks and a need for discussion before decisions. This grassroots tradition, born from operating under an illegal system, meant that the unions were filling a gap left by banned political parties. The exception was the illegal South African Communist Party whose members were active in these networks and in the wider movement as part of the ANC.

II   There was a link to the national democratic demands for the right to vote and to organise politically on an equal basis with whites. Black trade unionism meant a commitment to the ending of Apartheid – there was never any pretence that there was a split between the economic and the political.

III   A combination with the Black consciousness movement, requiring Black leadership in the movement.

When Black unions were reluctantly legalised by the white government in 1979, this made no impact on these three elements. The unions sought to combine in the Federation of South African Trade Unions (FOSATU) in the same year and started to coordinate actions with the Youth Wing of the ANC and other resistance elements. Efforts were intensified to create one organisation to represent all trade unions and as a result, in 1985 in Zambia over 30 trade unions joined together to form the Congress of South African Trade Unions (COSATU). Its first national actions were a direct challenge to the State. During the general election of 1987 COSATU organised a two-day 'stay away from work' as a protest over the denial of the right to vote. In July 1989, along with other resistance groups, they organised a National Defiance Day during which facilities reserved for whites only were invaded and taken over.

COSATU had national demands and organised and recruited workers around them. These were:

- To establish one union for each industry within six months.

- To focus on the exploitation of women workers.

- To call for the lifting of the state of emergency, withdrawal of troops from the townships and release of all political prisoners.

- To continue the call for international pressure, including disinvestment.

- To demand for the right to strike and picket.

- To determine a national minimum wage.

- To extend the struggle for trade union rights in the homelands.

The overlapping of both straightforward economic demands and overtly political ones helped to boost the struggle against Apartheid. It also established the trade union movement as a force not just for the workplace, but also for the common good. It is this element that movements in the Global South establish as part of their core message. Trade unions in many parts of the Global South take on many of the roles of wider social movements.

Islamic Socialism and the Organisation of Trade Unions

In the West we are very familiar with the alleged Christian roots of the Labour Movement. E.P. Thompson's monumental work, *The Making of the English Working Class* (1963), gives us a Marxist appreciation of how early trade unionism partly came out of its Methodist roots in the North of England. Mill workers and miners came away from preachers and turned to agitators, when heaven on earth became a union demand and not simply a pious hope for the

afterlife. This is no secondary factor as the ethical element to early
English Socialism – before the works of Marx and Engels – was clearly
taken from many of the Christian notions of the great movements
of the working class in England, Scotland, Wales and Ireland. The
Levellers, the Chartists and the Luddites were all movements
concerned with organisation, protest and justice on earth.

But what of other religious roots? In particular, the fastest
growing religion in the world, Islam? Global religions are mostly
seen through the prism of issues of equality on the progressive
side, or dismissed as almost mystical by reactionary elements.
As religion is conflated into racism, this is a nerve-wracking area
for white trade unionists from a Christian culture. There is also
the impact of Buddhism to consider in Myanmar, Cambodia
and Vietnam for example, and the role of Catholicism in the
Philippines, but for now Islam is the religion that has been pushed
into global centre stage.

Unbeknown to many there is actually a rich tradition and
thriving debate around the issue of Islamic Socialism. It is an
example to examine as the world is reacting to a combination of
pro-capitalist and often anti-Islamic forces. As trade unionists we
should embrace and be part of this debate, not in the abstract but
in looking at the material conditions of organising in Islamic states.
Islam is misrepresented across the world, misappropriated by
misogynists and racists to victimise workers and disrupt solidarity
between workers.

The debate includes discussion about how Islamic teachings
move into the essence of Socialism and trade unionism. The
emphasis on the rejection of usury for example, is cited as an
almost anti-capitalist teaching of Islam, whilst the notions of
Zakat (giving to charity) and fasting during Ramadan are based
on collective solidarity. But the more salient issues are about how
Muslim workers organise, and the extent to which it is in anyway
different. When looking at the organising of Call Centre workers
in Casablanca (*Our Trade Unions*), it was clear that the workers
used their existing material arrangements under Islam to organise
more effectively. For example:

- They would organise via spiderwebbing in women-only places as determined under Islam and around issues that women had identified – safe travel home for example. By meeting at women-only events, at women-safe spaces as allowed under Islam, they ensured no interference from mostly male managers.

- Events would not include alcohol and an emphasis was on welcoming and children-friendly activities, with food and drink.

- There is a strong ethical element to the meetings, often with prayers.

- There was an emphasis on collective solidarity and participation.

The Moroccan workers saw no contradiction between their trade unionism and their faith. Not all the workers shared the faith to the same degree, or some even at all, but all accepted the notions of how it applied to their campaign. These notions of Islamic Socialism are real in the Global South. Some Marxists in this tradition are Western-style Marxists who just happen to be Muslim. But there is also a tradition of transferring Islamic teachings into socialist conclusions, with writers and activists from India, Pakistan and Indonesia. Much of their work – from writers like Mushir Hosain Kidwai (an Indian lawyer and leader in the Pan-Islamic Society) – veers over into the ethical element of socialism, at the expense of the material basis of Marxism. But it is this aspect of the organised working class – through the power of arguments about ethics – that appears to have been almost completely forgotten in much of the West.

The persecution of Communists and trade unionists in countries like Iran and US-dominated Iraq is often the last word on Islam for many trade unionists. Coupled with the persecution and hostility towards women, the gay community, people with disabilities and the strict laws on alcohol and marriage in Saudi and other states, it can mean that many will walk away from any discussion about Islam and the Left. Yet the biggest persecution of Muslims and the Left took place in 1965, carried out by the state forces of the military and the Police. The mass murder of Communists, Socialists and trade unionists who were almost all Muslims in 1965 in Indonesia remains an event largely ignored in the UK or the rest of the West.

Indonesia is the largest Islamic economy in the world, with a workforce of 140 million workers and a population of 279 million. The Asian Tiger economy may have slowed down, but it remains one of the fastest growing and most robust capitalist markets in the world. Its social and political history is one of the most shocking in the world. Indonesia has its own tradition of what is termed 'Saraket Islam' (SI), which was the first mass movement in Indonesia. Formed in 1912 when Indonesia was still a Dutch colony, it evolved from being a largely middle-class organisation into a mass movement as it attracted the interest of workers and peasants who were organising into trade unions and into pro-independence and anti-colonial organisations. Amongst the many workers and peasants who joined were Communists and Socialists led by the trade union activist Semaun, who later became the first chairman of the PKI – the Indonesian Communist Party. The events of the Russian Revolution and the ending of the First World War impacted greatly on the Saraket Islam movement, radicalising its growing membership.

By the early 1920s Indonesian trade unions were organising strikes across the colony, disrupting the Dutch occupiers and winning wage increases. The tensions inside the SI were mostly due to the radical activity of these workers, and in 1920 the movement split with formation of the PKI. The split between the 'white faction' and the 'red faction' led to the severe decline of the SI. Its membership collapsed and its leadership sought to create the Indonesian Islamic Party in 1929, with its own internal dissent over attempts to cooperate with the Dutch colonial Regime.

The independence and anti-colonial struggle against the Dutch, and after that the war against the British, was led by these workers, many of whom were members of the PKI but were from an almost entirely Muslim population. Independence was achieved in 1949 after a four-year war against the Dutch (the Dutch were assisted in their war against the Indonesian people by the Royal Navy who provided naval cover and bombardments).

It is against this background that subsequent elections and failed coalitions finally led to the government of President Sukarmo, based on left reformism and an alliance with Islamic and military factions. Throughout the 1950s and up until 1965 this government introduced reforms and modernisation in health and education. This led to a number of proven Western interventions via the CIA and MI6, designed to overthrow the government. In 1965 there was a so-called protection coup led by leftists and involving the assassination of a number of Generals who were allegedly plotting to overthrow the government. This moment is now more widely understood as a 'false flag' operation in the tradition of the Reichstag Fire in Nazi Germany in 1933. It provoked an immediate military coup organised by the Military under the leadership of General Suharto, who kept Sukarmo under house arrest until 1967 when he installed himself as President, with the support of Islamic and military organisations.

The aftermath of this was the most appalling massacre of 1.2 million people, rounded up and executed by the Indonesian Government. So astonishing and so brutal was this genocide that it effectively destroyed the left for the next two decades. It remains the largest political massacre in history, supported and aided by the United States and the UK. Activists, members and supporters were persecuted across the country, executed by guns, swords, bamboo spikes, beheadings and drownings.

Today Indonesia has the fourth largest workforce in the world, with trade union density at about five percent. Trade union rights in the country are amongst the worst in the world. The parliamentary system is marked by the dominance of a pro-market party of modern neoliberals on one hand, and a more Islamic and nationalist party on the other hand – who are currently in government.

Yet trade unions have reorganised into a serious force in

Indonesia. After the economic crisis of 1999 finally led to the end of military dictatorship, the unions (who played little part in the downfall of the government) emerged in new competing federations. Still based on the organising tactics of SI and PKI traditions, they are re-establishing themselves. With a combination of the 'strategy from above and the strategy from below', they have successfully organised strikes across many important sectors in the economy. In October 2012 they led a General Strike involving 2 million workers utilising the 'sweeping tactic' similar to the role of flying pickets. But soon after this the trade union federations signed an agreement on industrial harmony. The constant threat to workers' jobs in Indonesia is the use of so-called 'footloose' companies that quickly relocate to Cambodia and Vietnam. This common global development is at the heart of many union-organising questions in Indonesia.

The experiences, knowledge and history of even great defeats like Indonesia are not fed into the UK and other Western movements. But the tragedies and the agonies of Indonesia tell us more about the positive role that Islamic organising had in the creation of the progressive left movement than we currently understand. Instead, we are fed a story of Islamic leaders turning on the people as though this was some purely Islamic affair. The role of the Dutch colonists, of the British military, the operations of the CIA and MI6 and the legitimacy given to the Suharto government even whilst it was slaughtering its citizens should all be up there in the lessons for trade unions in the UK.

Chapter 6
Rank and file power or shop floor power

NSIDE THE OFTEN INTROVERTED WORLD of the left, just saying 'rank and file power' is supposed to be an incontrovertible good. Everyone on the left believes in it, celebrates its achievements from the past and aspires to see it in the future. Who could disagree? There is not a General Secretary in the movement who would say 'I think members have too much say in what goes on inside the union'.

But what is it?

It used to look like lots of white men in big coats, voting by a show of hands at football grounds or in car parks to come out on strike. This image is prevalent in any news coverage of the UK in the 1960s and the 1970s. Intimidation at mass meetings, bully boys facing down anyone who didn't put their hands up, and then scenes of pushing and fighting the Police and sometimes each other on mass picket lines. Inevitably there would also be meetings in pubs and clubs.

There is a grain of truth in this. This style of trade union democracy would look so out of place now and actually in most sectors would be completely impossible to organise in this way. This is not to suggest that it was wrong then, but rather to state that this is not how unions would do it now. Nor should we want to. In effect it failed. By the end of the miners' strike it became clear that employers and the state now knew how to crush this style of trade unionism. With a national Police force, an orchestrated media vilification campaign and the use of draconian employment laws, it then became possible to at least contain the power of organised workers. Steel workers, miners, print workers and many others have experienced this.

In today's modern economy, summoning Deliveroo or Uber workers, online or hospitality workers to a big hall or open space to vote by hand would simply be impractical. Workers rarely exist in the type of big workplaces anymore. They are more isolated and dissipated, work very different patterns and approximately 3.5% of the UK workforce now have more than one job.

In this respect we must redefine what rank and file power is in a union and how it is organised. It is not the return of the 1970s organisational norms – car parks and mass meetings – but it is much more nuanced, subtle and based much more on technology, in order to facilitate democracy for all workers.

Where it does not differ is in its ability for members of the union to control the affairs of the union and to make its leaders and activists more accountable. It is this democracy that unions must engender if they are to sustain and grow membership.

Repeal the Anti Trade Union Laws

The first obstacle to rank-and-file power is the UK Employment Laws. They are condemned by the International Labour Organisation (ILO) and are considered to be the most draconian in Europe. They are designed to make it extremely difficult to organise industrial action (a human right under the UN Charter) and stack all the odds in favour of employers. There is a clear consensus that the only option is to call for all of them to be repealed. The work of the Institute of Employment Rights in detailing how and why this must be done cannot be bettered here – they have set out in precise legal detail what the arguments and options are (see www.ier.org.uk for more information).

These laws have massively impacted the ability of union members to organise themselves and assert some power over what happens in their trade union. The biggest and most hypocritical aspect of this is the requirement for full postal ballots for elections and industrial action. The impact of this requirement in the age of IT is indefensible. The effects are reductive:

■ They significantly slow down the process of organising. Unions have to give seven days' notice for ballots, have to realistically allow about three weeks for ballot papers to be posted out and returned, then to be counted by an independent service.

■ They then have to give 14 days' notice of any industrial action, meaning that at a minimum it will take a union nine weeks to organise action, assuming that they ignore any effort to negotiate or bargain a compromise in discussions.

■ It reduces turnout significantly, with elections lucky to achieve a 16% turnout, even for the position of General Secretary of a union.

■ Turnout in ballots for action, with the new 50% threshold rules, are also very difficult for unions to enhance, especially in scattered workplaces and national ballots.

■ Members often express impatience and dissatisfaction over this, at the union rather than at the law.

The use of online voting is an obvious necessity. Where unions are simply consulting members before a postal ballot or after an offer has been received, then very high turnout is much more easily achieved, representing better democracy and in a style that members are comfortable with and recognise. There is no evidence that it can be subverted or interfered with any more than a postal ballot can. The added advantage is of course that it can be done more quickly.

Which also leads us to the question of online meetings. There is a lot of anecdotal evidence that members like them, whether by Teams or Zoom. Logging on from home or work to hear a short report back, to hear and ask questions and to take part in an online poll have proved popular with some workers. It has enhanced participatory democracy.

This does not mean that it suits all workers in all situations. It is interesting that some online worker surveys have shown that one of the first things that many lone workers like to do is to meet up with other workers. It is also the case that there are workplaces where physical gatherings are still possible and efficient: depots, distribution centres, railways, post offices, schools, etc. The essence of spiderwebbing is the networking and lists of contacts that need to be used. All of this is simply enhancing the norms of the twenty-first century online life and using it to involve workers more in the workings of union life.

There are limits. The use of X/Twitter is still fraught with problems. It is not universally used and is unfortunately a place where people are open to abuse and racism. It is a platform designed for proclamations rather than discussion and debate. It cannot be a substitute for serious consultation and discussion, open as it is to all users and not just union members.

Unions are held back from increasing union member participation and control because they are not allowed to use these everyday methods.

The other massive impact of the anti-trade union laws is the banning of solidarity. This is an explicit element that must be repealed – but is the element that any government is unlikely to want to reduce. The outlawing of secondary action, from coming out in sympathy strikes, refusing to cross a picket line, the banning of flying pickets, or the absurd restriction on numbers of pickets effectively disempower trade unions. This banning of solidarity has severely weakened trade union actions and cut right across the cardinal principle of unity.

The revival of participation and solidarity by the removal of these laws is an essential part of rebuilding rank and file power.

Where is the alternative?

In recent times there have been many seminal political moments – for example the Brexit vote, the Black Lives Matter campaign, the cost-of-living crisis, the appalling treatment of immigrants and refugees and the issues related to the climate crisis. Massive debates have taken place about nationalisation, racism, nationalism, the NHS, the crisis in housing and the rise of child poverty. Trade unions often have good progressive positions on all these things, as they often represent the workers on the front line. But do these positions resonate with members or even get through to them?

The standard answer will be that these positions are often

produced after hard discussions at conferences or congresses. But the question is – how much does this matter anymore? Does it enhance member empowerment? The cost of UNISON annual conference to the union is nearing £10 million every year, similar in scale for other trade unions.

This is not to denigrate the need for Congress or Conference. There is a need for a place for branch delegates to meet and discuss policy, to debate and agree on the big questions. It is an essential part of the union life. But this has been the style and tradition for over a hundred years in the movement. Is it still fit for purpose?

The real absence of politics inside union workplaces is a factor negatively impacting rank-and-file organising power. In the 1970s it was clear that unions had workplace activists who would argue for anti-racism campaigns, an alternative economic strategy, about the 'Common Market' as it was called then, and about the defence industry and the cost of nuclear weapons. There are today still many thousands of activists in unions who raise politics. But unions now are a much smaller presence, with half the members of 1979, in an economy that is much bigger than 1979 with 3 million more workers.

We saw the impact of this in the Brexit vote. There was no socialist or trade union case for Brexit that was effectively raised in workplaces. There were some unions like RMT who put out a case, but beyond that it was difficult to find. Brexit essentially became a debate about racism, nationalism and immigration. There was not a trade union case for Brexit and nor would it ever be. But the lack of an activist base armed with arguments about the union case meant that this part of the debate over Brexit was crowded out. Consequently, the debate around EU austerity interventions in Greece and Portugal, the EU-led Transatlantic Trade and Investment Partnership (allowing companies the right to sue governments that don't put public service contracts out to tender) and the attacks on workers' rights, were all unheard.

The decline of union power seems to be linked to the decline of its political base. The progressive left forces have fled the field on many issues. The decline in numbers and the absence of big branch meetings in big workplaces is a mitigating factor in this. Working out cause and effect in this is difficult, given the many variations in workplace cultures and traditions. But looking outside the unions we see a number of factors that ought to encourage the unions to take up politics again:

■ The lack of differences between all the mainstream parties, compounded by the first past the post system. Many will see the solution in continuing to fight inside the Labour Party, others in looking at alternative candidates. Whether the unions like it or not, that is what voters are already doing.

■ The vast mobilisations taking place outside the unions. Young workers in particular whilst not joining trade unions are joining protests about Gaza, racism and global warming.

■ The lessons from the Global South are that a union requires a mixture of organising around national demands whilst mobilising local workers. India and South Africa are such examples. The idea from South Africa of the trade unions 'filling the spaces' left by political parties.

How unions do this is difficult. Political education and training are required, as well as link ups with campaigns and with the *Morning Star*, all helping to raise the profile of politics. But mostly it will be meaningless unless it is based on organisational and resource support for campaigns and a big effort to mobilise members and activists to turn out for the protests and events.

To illustrate this, we can see at a local level how this might work. On Merseyside there are a number of groups organising solidarity with the Palestinians. They achieve so much. There are weekly marches in the city, vigils and many other events. They have linked up with Arab communities in the city (it has the largest Arab community outside London) and are agitating around Barclays Bank and the Merseyside Local Government Pension Fund.

They have organised packed out public meetings and have sent coaches of supporters down to the London National marches. Only recently they collectively raised over £2,000 to donate to the Liverpool Mosque to cover the cost of coaches during Ramadan. The work of these local campaigners has been immense.

But it is unevenly matched by the trade union movement. The £2,000 raised came mostly from two unions – UNISON and UCU. The unions only occasionally seek to mobilise its members for marches or protests. We therefore have a contrast between the popularity and participation of people in the city, not just in the Muslim community but also amongst young people, and the response from parts of the movement. In South Africa COSATU talked about 'filling the spaces left by political parties' – here is some idea of what they were talking about. At a Palestinian Rally organised in Preston by Michael Lavalette (the local Stop the War campaigner and a trade union activist now standing as an independent parliamentary candidate), the question was put to the 7,000 people in the crowd – 'put your hand up if you are a member of a trade union'. Roughly less than one in ten did. The crowd was urged to immediately join a trade union.

There is no doubt that the impact of a recent public letter from the General Secretary of Unite about Palestine has been overwhelmingly negative. The letter was an attack on the anti-war movement, based on the notion that Unite membership based in the defence industry should determine the union position on ending arms sales to Israel. The contrasting lack of anything to say about the genocide involving the families of some members of Unite (they have a substantive Palestinian membership) is indicative of a political weakness. Unite is not the only union to have been silent on the genocide, but it is the most high-profile.

The unions should follow the example of the Global South in raising national questions and political demands. This would mean many more tensions with Labour MPs and with employers, and it may lead to active internal opposition, but by reducing their ethical and moral standing they will not avoid their continued decline, especially amongst young workers.

Resources for Organising

Much of this debate has already been covered in *Our trade Unions* and it would serve no purpose to repeat it here. Other than to say that not only are resources an issue for union growth, but they also impact upon the empowerment of members and the rank and file.

Organising workers – even as set out by the US 'gurus' – has as an explicit aim: the empowerment of the members. Whilst this is often set out as power in relation to the employers, an obvious necessity, it also plays out as power inside the union. This is often a source of tension, conflict and even the eventual decline of union power.

Where workers are involved in a dispute, especially if they are new members, then they go through a confusing, frustrating, and often demoralising process of learning. Some see it as an opportunity for personal growth – which is not really the point – and will be diverted off into union jobs or HR careers, but most will find it a revealing and complicated experience. In relation to the union there are often many disappointments to be had. Many of these are resource-related and so can have a negative impact on organising and the confidence that members have in the union. But you can't build a rank-and-file empowered membership without resources. They need:

■ Control over resources, with quick and easy access to decision makers or the ability under rule to have their own funds and the ability to allocate them.

■ Swift access to lists and other data on their members, access to research on their sector and their employer.

■ The efficient and meaningful right to challenge decisions made above their head and without consultation with them.

■ Proper access to rules and guidance on internal union processes.

■ Full discretion in their union messaging to members.

Members find it surprising how little autonomy they have and how much power 'gatekeepers' inside the organisation may have over their ability to take action, spend money and speak out. The impact of this on many activists has been to disillusion them. 'Unions are a racket' is one phrase that has been used by a disillusioned activist.

Unions who proclaim themselves 'member-led' need to ensure that this is the case. A union must be member-led and be seen to be member-led. That is the issue with resources.

SUMMARY

THE UNIONS ARE IN A BETTER PLACE than they were in January 2022 when the 800 P&O workers were sacked and offered re-engagement on much worse terms. Most of them refused and actually the majority of them were not in a union. There was very little the union could or did do for them anyway. The equivalent now is the announcement of the loss of 1600 jobs in the steelworks in Port Talbot. Whether the unions can do much more this time around is yet to be seen. But they have been balloted as noted earlier and public sympathy for trade unions is reflected in the strength of the support for them.

In summary we can list some indicators to help unions regroup and reorganise in order to reap the benefits of what the members have done by striking in 2022/23.

Many unions have retreated from face-to-face contact with members. This is a major issue which must be resolved by organising. Members like to meet and see the union and to them the union is personified by local activists. Anything that puts this at the heart of organising revival is a major change.

Key unions lost membership density in Thatcher and Blair years and adjusted their structures to manage decline. But they now try to manage growth without having changed their structures. We cannot 'squeeze in' new workers and young workers into organisations that are based on the old economy and the old ways. Unions have to reform how they are organised. All the ways of committees, meetings, conferences and congresses have to be changed to suit workers with more than one job, with flexible working arrangements, with less time and with access to smart technology.

The decades of unemployment and employer offensive meant that the activists and shop steward base of the unions has been massively reduced. In many workplaces even with members there are no representatives. This impacts massively on workplace power and democracy.

The best organised sections of unions should seek to recruit through the supply chain and on surrounding industrial estates. This requires flexibility and resources that the union must pool, as currently none seem able to match the scale of the task with the means required. Unions must cooperate, not compete.

All shop floor and so-called rank and file initiatives must be focused on workplaces and issues and not be dominated by internal union wrangles and elections. Broad Lefts have become overwhelmingly introspective dealing with the union rather than the member/worker at work.

The spiderwebbing style is well within the tradition of revolutionaries and activists in unions, it is particularly user-friendly for young workers and those with no experience of trade unionism.

The big unorganised sectors and the big employers are ripe for organising. This is the challenge for the unions. These sectors and employers are outside the union hinterland, they are beyond the existing areas of membership. But Amazon workers have shown a way forward in Coventry, the Deliveroo workers in London, Uber workers and many others are organising themselves in many cases. The onus is on the trade unions to meet this challenge. At the moment the unions are not institutionally and structurally up to this challenge.

Yet the unions have achieved so much since 2022. They have raised the wages of millions of workers during the worst cost of living crisis since the 1970s, defended jobs and terms and conditions and finally made space for the case against the privatised utilities, railway companies, and the way that much of the UK economy is organised around precarious work. That is quite a success in itself.

They have also impacted on politics and the debates about public life. Whether it is UCU and NEU on Education, UNISON on public services, Unite on general cost of living increases or RMT on the state of the railways, the unions have a voice that they didn't have in 2021. That is thanks to union members.

Unions continue to be on the right side of the arguments about corruption, greed and dishonesty in public life, and are deemed to be separate in most cases from that political class that people distrust and are repulsed by. It is to their great credit that the unions are still clearly on the side of the people when all other institutions – Parliament, the Police, the BBC, the newspapers, the utility companies, universities, the education system, the railway owners and football club owners – have proved themselves to be sickeningly broken.

There is every reason to be optimistic that they will now move to even higher ground – with increased membership, more power and the advantages of a democratically-empowered membership. Organising was always the key and mistakes have been made.

If the unions are to grow again and become the voice of the working class once more, it is now at least in their hands. They have to recruit many more young workers, recruit in more parts of the private sector, they have to organise in new ways and they have to sustain their growth over a long period of time.

One day a General Secretary will be a woman who worked in McDonalds, Uber or Amazon, who has maybe worked in social care or as a delivery rider with Just Eat. That will make a difference if it means that those workers in those sectors of the economy are completely unionised and a core part of the union movement, with global solidarity and unity at its heart.

It would be apt to finish with the famous quote from the Indian leader of the Grunwick Strikers Jayabean Desai, who personified the internationalism of trade union struggle, when leading a two-year strike by mostly East African Asian workers over union recognition. Her quote could apply to many workplaces in the UK today:

'*What you are running here is not a factory, it is a zoo. In a zoo there are many animals. Some are monkeys who dance on your fingertips, others are lions who can bite your head off. We are those lions, Mr Manager*'

To all the lions everywhere, our day will come.

— Nigel Flanagan April 2024

Order *African Uhuru* here:

manifestopress.coop

AFRICAN UHURU: THE FIGHT FOR AFRICAN FREEDOM IN THE RISE OF THE GLOBAL SOUTH BY ROGER MCKENZIE

African Uhuru: the fight for African freedom in the rise of the Global South – Roger Mckenzie's latest writing – addresses several distinct but complementary audiences.

In focussing on the radical tradition of African self liberation he draws attention to the most dynamic aspect of the decolonisation process, the unstoppable impetus to overthrow the shackles of imperial domination and traverse the path to full liberation on terms set by Africa's people themselves.

That this process was intimately involved with global processes – the Russian revolution; the defeat of fascism; the Latin American drive to national sovereignty against the dominant imperium; the Chinese fight to end foreign domination; the national liberation movements of South Asia – draws our attention to the singular, particular and heroic aspects of the movement for African liberation.

For a British audience the anti-colonial struggles of the peoples of Africa and the Caribbean are contested territory with a powerful attempt by contemporary ideologues of empire to erase the role of slavery and super exploitation in the creation of modern Britain.

YOURS FOR THE REVOLUTION - THE EVOLUTION OF TOM MANN'S POLITICAL THOUGHT
BY PHIL KATZ

Tom Mann remains Britain's most accomplished trade unionist but each generation has to rediscover him.

With the current union upsurge his time has come round again.

Mann's theory of socialism and class organisation was literally forged in the fiercest and most decisive union battles, extending over a fifty year period. Yet little is known of his activity in the last two decades of his life, when he had his greatest impact and most enduring influence.

This was recognised throughout Europe, China, Australia, the USA and the Soviet Union. "Yours for the revolution" will fascinate and inspire. It covers his major strikes, organisations and the evolution of his political thought.

It makes for vital reading for those seeking a path to socialism today..

WINGED WORDS

Edited by

Heather Killingray

First published in Great Britain in 2003 by
POETRY NOW
Remus House,
Coltsfoot Drive,
Peterborough, PE2 9JX
Telephone (01733) 898101
Fax (01733) 313524

HB ISBN 1 84460 944 8
SB ISBN 1 84460 945 6

FOREWORD

Although we are a nation of poets we are accused of not reading poetry, or buying poetry books. After many years of listening to the incessant gripes of poetry publishers, I can only assume that the books they publish, in general, are books that most people do not want to read.

Poetry should not be obscure, introverted, and as cryptic as a crossword puzzle: it is the poet's duty to reach out and embrace the world.

The world owes the poet nothing and we should not be expected to dig and delve into a rambling discourse searching for some inner meaning.

The reason we write poetry (and almost all of us do) is because we want to communicate: an ideal; an idea; or a specific feeling. Poetry is as essential in communication, as a letter; a radio; a telephone, and the main criterion for selecting the poems in this anthology is very simple: they communicate.

CONTENTS

A Deeper Awareness

When you look, with what,
Do you see?
When we feel, do we really know
All that the world could be?

If we had no senses, what a state.
No way of knowing, only inner space.
All that we know, gone.
Only inner realms of being
To substantiate.

There'd be no time.
One day would last
An eternity.
Complete and utter bliss.
Or a perpetual state of agony?

So, how do we really
Know that all we
Perceive is real?
Do our senses tell
A lie?
Have they the ability
To measure everything
In being?

All these structures that we build,
Technology, high into the sky.
What would they now be,
If our senses to perceive their reality
Were denied?

Elizabeth Haruna

SANS AMOUR

These days our dreams fall down broke and unloved
An ugly mirror view washed down with a half-pint of Scotch
I wonder where you are when the winds howl your name
Like a ship without port you just sailed away

Now those memories burn like cheap absinthe in Prague
Drank with her hair and a book of dead crows
Do you pray for me when I'm alone in my bed
Or dodging the raindrops that fall overhead?

I beg for that day the sky spits you back out
When you float downstream on a tattered storm cloud
As we grasp tight freedom's rotting hand
And swim towards the moon's reflection

But like a ghost ship lost at sea you just sailed away
My beautifully haunted Amélie.

Chris Brownsword

MM

M ankind
I n his
L ust for wealth
L eeches the Earth's
E cology
N either knowing
N or caring
I f he
U ses up its resources before the next
M illennium.

Alison Batcock

INVISIBLE

How loud the silence in the crowd,
Talking out aloud
The quietest and the still
Stands alone invisible
'See me,' she shouts
'I am here,'
Who can see the lady grey
Standing alone invisible.

Annette Blake

DEAR LATEST

So mad,
So bad
of you to lie to me.
So sad that your voice is so transparent
for I am only playing games with myself,
not you.
You were just a speck on the horizon,
(perhaps a seagull, flying away from me),
but the game was a house I lived in.
I wanted you to live there too
and pretend, like me
it was real.

Alison Booth

THE SADDEST THING

He is everywhere.
He is in my thoughts.
He is everything.
To me.

The reason for existence.
The reason that I breathe.
I need him
Just
To be.

But . . .

The saddest thing
Is that I know
He's never noticed
Me.

Joanne Borrill

THE UNGODLY FLOWER

Long and strong, their grey stems tower high above the grey roofs,
their white flowers uniformly the same except for the central one,
which commands the rest.

No insect will spread the nectar of these flowers,
for only the birds of the air, can see into their blooms,
but some of their number will not perch.
They seem to know it is not a Godly thing they see.

Made by men to snare their fellow man in a net of illumination
but its light is not to show the way.
It is to corner and capture, to help keep man confined to his box.
No wonder the birds of the air steer clear.

Martin Brogan

PUTRID CIRCUS

In dark capital alleys he clutches his Gladstone,
Full of the knives that cut light out,
Reaches in and draws the shiniest, honed to the hilt.
Look at me in the name of dog,
I will clean these Sodom streets.

The dark, soot-stained bricks hardly cast a shadow,
Camouflaged by smog-iced air and dark attire.
But, now he steps into the light,
His shadow top hat and cane-carrying long,
Black ground-touching cape drags in gaslit pools.

Now he listens for fair gendered footsteps,
His heart beating in time with approaching heel and toe.
The knife-cutting silence hears the lamp gas hiss,
Like a knighthood of vampires.
Empty cobbled street stays mum, unable to warn of impending danger,
Houses beg voice to scream 'go no further,
But they sit inanimate in their rigid stony shame.

She has plied her bawdy trade,
Helped through by the penny-a-pint mother's ruin,
Looks old like unwashed rags, but young as modern child.
Hardship has been her closest ally, no easy days.
No life will wield its final blows.

Her last streetwalk now, gripping her latest shilling,
Snuffed by the internecine pike that swallows life,
Extinguished by the lamplighter who determines light or dark.
Victorian victim of the pleasures of man.
A rag doll in life's putrid circus.

The rage commenced after the first downwards stroke,
Ending only in his tiredness of limb.
Evil has conquered innocence yet again, again.
Now they have both left, dripping in puddles,
Him with a shadow, her with none.

Ian Bowen

BRIDGES

Sweet and sour emotions
And another new devotion,
Breathing in and out a sigh,
Enough to make you want to lie.

Tight skirt and shiny top,
No way that it can stop.
Behind my back, my arms and hands,
In my mind, making plans.

In the window myself I see,
Do not even recognise me,
But I feel the way I should,
Found myself, you know I could.

Gill Buckmaster

PRAISE FOR PARTIES!

Sombre winter signals the need
to celebrate, revere our spirit
that will triumph over this cold season
with the energy of joyous life.

The buzz of talk, shallow or deep
sparks recognitions, insight of individuals
though different or even opposed
but linked in the joy of expression
not just in words, dress, jokes -
in glances, nods, winks, laughs.

Signals flick with judgements
suspended in the humility of defects,
hopefully improvable, tolerable
or pardonable in the party mode.
On to the next event!

Fleming Carswell

HELLO!

Was that a knock at the door?
No it's all in my head
A phone call for me?
No I'm a misdialled number

If I cry will you hear me?
If I laugh will you laugh too?
I wish I could hide but if no one knows I am here
How will they know I've gone?

What is existence?
If something exists people know about it
And acknowledge it
Do I exist?

Hello!

Anna-Marie Clarke

RUSTY

Last Saturday morning
We took Rusty along
To be put down;
He didn't look back once
Nor seemed to mind
As they led him away
Slowly; for he was lame
And very nearly blind.
We swallowed hard,
Consoled ourselves:
Being cruel to be kind.

It's strangely quiet
This Monday morning
In our street;
No ritual barking
As the postman tramples
Gravel underneath.

Denis Donnelly

SOLITUDE

O quietness I yearn for thee,
O stillness is it thee I seek?
In that place where solitude abides
And no one dareth speak.

O solitude where is thy abiding-place
Where peace and stillness dwells?
Is it where the eagles soar
Or where I walk the fells?
I have searched the highest mountain peak,
I have roamed the whole world wide
To find thy place, (that none doth know),
Where solitude doth hide.

'Keep searching seeker, do not despair,
For whilst thou seekest I am there,
But if thou endest thy quest for me,
I, solitude, shall be lost to thee'.

Solitude art thou my friend,
My bosom companion, my partner for life?
'Yes!' it doth whisper in my ear,
'I am all that and more;
For I am the gateway to
Unrealised peace, tranquillity, rest;
See! There am I through yonder door.'

I pushed the door at its request
And found myself o'er come with rest,
The peace of untold ages mine!
But hearken, friend, I left behind
All those things that weighed me down;
The heavy heart, the sour faced frown.

The burdens, in life - time's sack
accumulated, all had disappeared.
And as I lay me down in the arms of solitude,
Peace, comfort, silence, replaced
All that I once feared.

David Eccles

THE TOWN

Stony town
Sometime never
Sandy layered
Every day

Dusty people
Dressed in rag
Bedraggled shrouds
Drenching rain.

Timeless stones
Struggling dogs
Coated layers
Roasted hogs

Flealess bitch
Fearful fangs,
Children feeding
Dead men hang

The bearded goat
Sometimes dancing
Heated stones
Fires enchanting

Sweated clamours
In lodges sick
Burning flesh
Making bricks

Clapping rhythm
Tapping sticks
Whirling layers
With dusty flicks

At the
Kasbar
Everyday

Gather round
Gather round

Alf Dimmock

STRANGFORD HERRINGS

A feast of herring in Portaferry
a day of green and golden walks
a happy day for a happy boy
but now I'm conscious something's lost
and I wonder what it is
on the water on the lough
where the whirlpool sleeps its silence
in the mouth of Strangford lough

A child's lost vision leaves me
how the years can disappear
my kids are smiling freely
and I'm glad that they are here
and they're innocent of the danger
on the water on the lough
where the whirlpool sleeps its silence
in the mouth of Strangford lough

The tribal shores are chanting
flags and emblems fly the mast
casting nets of hatred
they'll be loyal to the last
and their rhythms echo eerily
on the water on the loch
where the whirlpool sleeps its silence
in the mouth of Strangford lough

sowing seeds our sons' destruction
the fatal brew's reaction's near
my children and I we will be leaving
I'm glad they'll never feel the fear
of the brutal amongst the beauty
on the water on the lough
where the whirlpool sleeps its silence
in the mouth of Strangford lough.

George Engelen

DAD

Your stubble made prints on my cheeks
As I nestled on your chest,
Stale smoke poured from your breath
So sweet to me.

We'd sit on steps and watch the rain
Then splash our way home.

My heart stopped the day you left
Our rain turned to ice.

Like a jack-in-the-box
I waited,
For the lid to be unleashed,
Release me from darkness,
Pop up,
See the sun
If only for a minute.

But no one came to release the lid
That crushed me down daily.

I looked for answers in my little dark box
But all I found were memories.

Now older and wiser I look back
And see your pain.

Now you are no longer
'Dad'
Just a picture on Mum's dresser.

Susan English

STRENGTH

Strength is within you
Strength is always there,
Something you rely on
In sadness and despair;
Like hope it keeps you going,
Like hope it always will,
But don't take it for granted
Because you may fall ill.
The one thing to rely on,
Whene'er your strength may fail
Is hope; hope, the only thing
Which always will prevail.

Sylvia Evans

THE COUNTDOWN YEARS

Mitres lean
towards assenting halos,
phoenix dream
of spires ascend.

Scant reward for
speculation of years
spent
in seminal invention.

Twisted castors
on mosaics of
portending stars,
foretelling tea-dreg
certainties,
the whorl of thumb
impressions on the abyss
of banister directions:
stepping down
the stair-rod years.

Michael Alan Fenton

SO HAPPY

After several years of searching,
Of looking all around,
I believe I've finally succeeded
I've discovered much happier ground.

I've never yet felt so happy,
I've been helped up from being down,
By someone who is more than special
Who has turned my life around.

I lie there while he caresses me
Revelling in all that I've missed
And when we first got together,
It was as if I'd never been kissed.

For his kisses are calming and magical,
Releasing my cursed spell,
That was cast upon me some time ago,
It took away my trust as well.

I'd had bad times with others,
But now, he's put that right,
I let myself go when I'm with him,
He is such a wonderful delight!

Here's to our future together -
At last all's good and well,
I'll devote my whole self to him,
As he's helped me come out of my shell.

Adele Gwinnett

THE LIFE OF A LOVE

She lived passionately, sweetly, dreaming
In my head; gentle kisses on my palm
But I pulled away. She moved gracefully,
Sensually through my world, waiting
For my smile - patiently, fatally, willingly.

She touched me, lush tender hands
In mine, lips pressed to my chest
Hair caressing me, burying my
Betrayal - smelling of promise and life.

She welcomed my attention with devotion
And deference, bathing in masked
Emotion, allowing me to overpower her
With a commitment to the cause.

Fatalist that she was, with the
Optimism of youth we danced, bathed
In colour from her dangerous rouged lips
And my pale, captured face;

Until the demure image, with her
Lascivious twinkling eyes overcame
Any doubts - enfolding that feeling.
She lived wonderfully and brightly
In my mind; soft terrible tears, falling

To wash my hand as she turned her back.

Tom Garbett

UNTITLED

I'm breathing for life
Breathing to the last
For the last life, lost

For the disused bingo hall on Black Prince Road
Stone-dead and cold

For the soldier young and army old holed up high in the cube-block
towers left towards Elephant

Low-sky lethargy south past the Oval
Brixton Road buildings still and silent, old bones in numbered graves

Back to the world and up through Loughborough Junction
Back views off the train tracks, thin dusk blue through
the even-spaced estates
Empty spaces, solid space, hollow
Like negative casts of the red-door blocks and the yellow-door blocks
and the blue-door box-block broken doors in line and time and again
High empty concrete, metered high, motionless
Emotions lost on the uniform floors, the eleventh floors,
fifth floors, sevenths
Augmented and diminished
Faltering Christs in frozen ascension, funnel of light now a tunnel of
concrete slats and strip lights
Life-tied. Ground broken

And I'm breathing to the end, to the urgent engines
Blacked-out windows, break-beats, brass-blasts gold on
Coldharbour Lane
Time condensed at the junction of the train tracks
Aimless energy travelling in life-lines
Down from the high-rise greys to the mortal noise

Breathing and the sad world dying
No start and no finish in handed-down time
Toxins and oxide wash
Breathing for the loss, for the hereditary line

I'm breathing for good, for the unbearable bones
For the loners, unillusioned
For the ongoing life

Corin Golding

JUNE THE 21ST

An observer looking up today
could see the spiked mine cases of conkers
waiting already in June trees.
By the embankment, a stiff green blackberry
is buttoned in every bramble flower,
sycamore keys are lemon lanterns.
Yet this is the longest day
when town front gardens are sporting roses.
Tomorrow the waning begins.

There has been a great washing of flags,
flung like tablecloths from upstairs windows.
Now, while Israeli guns probe to right
and left, menacing as Daleks,
the flags are being folded.
It's a bloodshot sunset upon
Jewish and Palestinian streets tonight.
Tanks take second place upon our English News,
relegated by the anguish of football.

A beautiful Arab woman fills her fridge
with medicine. Fingers fumbling in fear.
Here we have stockpiled lager and talk of despair.
Fewer pairs of cuckoos officially breed in Sussex,
another year's chance to hear one is all but gone.
They are putting up posters for the plays of autumn.
No evening will be quite as light again,
this side of winter for us
and never for some.

Anne Howard

MIRRORS

Here I stand, looking at you,
Thinking of times past,
And present.
Waiting, wishing and praying that
The clock would turn once again
Back to a past
Or shape a different present.

Glimmers of light in the darkness.
A well of strength forms from which to draw and drink.
Opportunities abound in the black still night.
But turn away: for none wish to see
the reflection of pain
of the change that is to be.
Disturbing the present and the past.

Here stands Truth.
In the glow of the light that filters through.
More questions. Now: await your response.
But there is no warmth of breath upon which words might dance
Nor lightness of touch.
No sound at all.
Just silence.

Still: you and I await Time.
For an opportunity lost.
Tears may be shed.
But the light will dawn.
And you and I trust
In the moonlight.
One.

Karen Hyman

Past It

He sits and mopes
And gazes and hopes,
The telly is his god,
At footy, golf, rugby too,
He used to be a sod,
Just sits and drools,
With can in hand,
Gazing at the screen,
Thinking of that far off time,
When he was in his teens,
Reluctant to move,
He calls for food,
He shouts, 'Where is my dinner?'
It's only at home he can gripe and whine,
'I used to be a winner!'

H Irving

THINKING OF YOU

In the morning when you're sleeping,
At lunchtime wondering if you're eating,
Hoping you're comfortable or are you in pain,
We think about you often.

In the afternoon questioning are you awake?
Do you need company or content as you are?
At teatime asking ourselves if you're hungry?
We think of you often.

We want to take you out and about,
Make you smile and your wishes come true,
To make you happy and remove your worries,
We think of you often.

Dearest Janet we feel for you always,
Wishing we could help in some small way,
To lighten your load and bring laughter your way,
We think of you often.

If there's anything you want or need,
Don't hesitate to ask we're all here ready,
To take you anywhere you want to go,
We're thinking of you often.

Jackie Kirk

DARKNESS

Waking at four
With the black dog at your shoulder.
In the cold still night
At the hour when the dead depart.

I think of two men
Who thirty years ago
Challenged each other
As if I were the dung heap
And they the cocks.

Now neither lifts the telephone
To tell me about their lives.
Their mothers die
Their wives disintegrate
The rites of time revolve.
So much was shared in the past
Now nothing is.

And the cold darkness at four
Creeps in my heart.
Its icy hand shakes me.
The brave front
Of this stiff edifice
Drops bricks from its facade.

Of course, yes, of course
Quite alright, thank you.
Just forget that you forget.
But the cold water beckons
In the still of the dawn.
And it is darkness that is breaking at the break of the day.

Chris Madelin

GALLOPING PEACE

I thought that I could
Gallop towards peace,
Outrun the black cloud gathering behind
But
                    It billowed before me filled with hate,
recrimination and political whataboutery.

I thought that I could
Kick up enough dust to let it settle on
A new convergence of the minds waiting behind
the mountains of traditions.

I thought that I could
wheel and turn
the other cheek
But
                    Still remain astride
      Riding towards a new dawn
Of an orange sunset brightening a green landscape
But
                    As I gallop through
The beauty before me dazzles and

I fall

To rise again
bathed in the rainbow.

Madeline McCully

LOVE AND HATE

I love my cat and my garden
I love to see her asleep on my rug.

I hate other folk's cats in my garden
Scratching up all that I've dug.

I hate other folk's cats in my garden
Sometimes I wish they were part of my rug!

Rocky Moon

DAYS GONE BY

The clothes are scrubbed and hung out to dry
Potatoes peeled and waiting to boil
Ironing piled high needing a press
Children screaming and making a mess
Muddy knees and smiling faces
Chocolate cakes and Sunday roast
In the oven ready to make
Old man shaved and pulling up braces
Down the pub for a couple of beers
Popping back later
For a snooze in the chair
Holy socks waiting for another patch over
Father's trousers cut down to fit
Stitched and ready to try on for size
Nothing wasted and nothing thrown away
All has its purpose and is put to good use
A penny earned is a penny saved
For desperate times
When fixing and altering have no use
However did we survive
In days gone by?

Zena Samuels

TWO SWALLOWS

We can sit alone at the breakfast table
I can watch you swallow down your food
Slowly and with dignity.

The summer sun can rise in the sky
And make us sweat in the afternoon
The swallows may fly to and from their nest.

But one thing sure between you and I
Though we compare to the birds in the sky
Two swallows don't make a summer.

Noel Thaddeus Lawler

OCEAN! OCEAN!

You light up a cigarette as I'm swept ashore and walk
holding hands with my envy toward the celestial gates
of the Bay of Bengal . . . My tongue twitches in fury
like the bitch of a winter all around as the sand and the
salt and the tears of the ocean rise like litany in unison . . .
You run into me somewhere near the waterfront
where the beach lies cobble-stoned and panting in season . . .
Your eyes move from green to grey to blue as the waves
like mermaids heave their breasts in climax . . .
Our eyes water as your cigarette smoke is blue
against the blue ocean when my envy and I walk in
silent camaraderie towards no tomorrow's.

Prasenjit Maiti

CHANGES

The world is changing
All around us
Second by second
Day by day
We may not see it
But as every second goes by
A second of our world is changing.

There's new lives born each day
And lives are taken away,
New trees grow and grow,
But old ones die and go.
Children grow older each day
And decide it's time, to move away.
Weather is changing each season,
But there is no particular reason.
Recycling takes place, and made into new,
Bottles, boxes and plastic, are just a few.
Businesses open, and take on work,
But at the same time, others are closing.
Pollution is released into the air,
Which damages part of our world.

Think about what we're doing
To our world!

Steff Martin

IF I COULD SING YOUR SONG

If I could sing your song,
It would be so beautiful.
For you radiate a beam
That sends its rays far and wide.
So bright that none could hide,
For it would find them.
Just knowing you is being blessed.

Your song would have a magic air,
And raise the hope of those in deep despair.
The melody would bring them light,
Darkness again disperse,
Hearing the brightness in every verse.

'Twould be as though the angels were singing,
Sweet beauty their voices ringing.
Such sounds no other could sing.
Your song indeed, a beautiful thing.

Grace Maycock

PERDITA'S GARDEN
(In memory of my late father)

Perdita's garden isn't much, it boasts no well kept lawns and such,
No loving hands will tender seedling sow, no nightingales,
caressed, or stately view.
But whispers in the grass abound, for here, much insect life is found.
And here, she felt, was safety, when from out some thoughtless door
was Perdi sent
The Lost One.
Home forever barred and hers no more,
A sanctuary then, was what she sought.
A place where none disturb her, where her
daughters could be raised.
Kitten Charm, a silver tabby, bright as any star
And little Gypsy Girl, coal black,
Her father's child. Peeping from some haven,
not too far, from Mother.
Gentle Perdi, who found friends and love
and warmth once thought forever lost.
They say when one world ends, another beckons,
Perdita, you gave me friendship and you showed your children,
that not all who stand erect are hard and cold.
Ere summer's haze was done, we walked as one.
I never go into your garden without thinking of you all.
Your little garden isn't much, but sweet violets grow
With dainty hue
I walk into your garden, and I think of you.

Susan Lickley

DARK NIGHT

Deep is the night
That crawls into day,
Into night
And back to day.

And deep are the thoughts that
Condescend to enter
The mind of the one
Suspended
In the halfway point
Between night and day.

And bold is the one
Who interferes;
For reason and logic
Have been superseded
By the strongest desire
To be left alone
Unsought,
Unfound,
Too deep to understand.

Maureen Penny

STATE OF CONSCIOUSNESS

Stop! I stand quiet
Like an ornamental statue, established to watch the world go by.
Peace falls like delicate snow over the space around me,
Making everything that went unnoticed before cry out.
Taking a breath, I breathe in a piece of time,
I retain it for a second before letting it escape as a fragment of history.

Kirstie Eleanor Mason

BELFAST

Green hills, not so far away, but close to where we used to play
School yard, the entry, winding streets,
Where once was heard the children's feet.

Now taking their place is Apartment blocks,
Newly built around the docks
Progress is what they call it, prosperity - we believe
But memories of those bygone years, will always mean more to me.

Elizabeth Ann Armstrong

THERE'S ALWAYS BLOODY ONE!

What am I?
Alone.
In a room with a view and a phone.
What are you?
You are the object of my desire
But you set your face on fire.

See over there,
On the shelf above the ocean,
She dances with people she knows
Yet doesn't.

Are you blind?
She calls you.

Your face has melted a bit.
The pink puddle on the floor says it all.

Anyone else would have went to her.
Anyone else would have talked.

But there's always bloody one!
Isn't there?

Cyra Armstrong

FORGOTTEN

A house with rage instead of laughter,
A house with darkness instead of light,
Broken picture frames photos slashed,
Torn paper, broken glass.
A voice shouts, a fist is raised,
A child cowers, shielding his face,
The effort is futile the fist strikes
The boy crumples.

A forgotten soul surrounded by hate
Silently his tears flow.

Sarah Appleby

To Work In Winter

Beams of yellow adorn my dwelling
Superimposed and crosshatched with more
Insects crawling on identical journeys
Destinations differ, traffic flows.

Dancing warily round the static
Moving objects taking care
Whole world of physics and machinery
Overtaking nature's way.

Villages fleet past grime streaked windows
Curves and camber, curbs and lights
People stepping in slow motion
Flashed past; gone, into the night.

Hands and feet that move in unison
Head that swivels round in time
Just to catch that car's intention
Weld it to my inner rhyme.

Prompt arrival is the daydream
More by luck than my desire
Let sleep this metal cage of action
Reliable old heap of mine.

Christine Ashurst

A Free And Fair Trial For Krishna Maharaj

Eastern Eye, April, two thousand and two
Published their article just for you.
Your lawyer Clive Stafford Smith
After 200 capital cases is
Utterly convinced of your innocence.
Peter Bottomley MP supports
300 parliamentarians' reports
With former Attorney General Nicholas Lyell
All facts were not aired in a free and fair trial.
President George Bush opposed the recount
53 years! A prodigious amount!
Reprieved from Deathrow in Florida Pen
Lead Defence Lawyer Benedict Kuene
Blocked from presenting evidence again
Placing Maharaj 40 miles away then.
Prosecutor Sally Weintraud calls
For a lethal injection to end it all!
Officer Gene Scott bought the bullets
Mark Chapman used to shoot John
Lennon Ex Beatle who used to sing song.
Pardon your majesty, does your hubby snore
Do you want to make peace or rather have war?
For the former please answer, we've had enough
Of your MI5 and 6's paranoid stuff
January thirty-first 1999
That marked Ford Escort police car
Two forty five PM was the time.
PC Deseta of Hayle Police Station knows
The B3302 near Cornwall's Leedstown's
'A Long Winding Road'. Re: Specs Mrs Bryant.

Jësu Ah'so

UNREQUITED

If I told you the truth would you turn and run
Or would you be proud to say we belong
The slightest touch or a simple smile
Makes my heart expand with joy
Why can't you see what you do to me?
When we're together my fears just melt away
And yet you insist on giving your heart to her
Leaving my hopes to crumble and die
You're kind and gentle to all you know
Which leads our friendship to blossom
You're there for me in every way but one
The one to make my happiness complete
Why do you love her so?
Why choose her and not me?
My heart aches when we are close
I long to reach out and touch
Smell your hair in my hands
Taste your kisses upon my lips
Your presence intoxicates my being
You're on my mind from first thing until last
Sometimes in your messages I think you feel the same
If only my hopes were true
To have you here within my arms
Would mean you love me too!

Natalie Clarke

FATHER

You worked hard all your days
In that uniform to please,
For you were in your need
And they laid down the law,
For Slaves need their Masters
And Masters need their Slaves
Until one dies or both.
And in-between you drank your wine
To kill the boredom and the pain
And the failure you felt within.
But you maintained a home
And fed the woman in your life
And the children from your wife.
(For them you could not do much)
And you worried about your health
And all the unpaid bills,
But at least you had your work
In that uniform to please.
And now all duties done
And resting in leisure's arms
With the toil of labour's days
Still pouring down your face,
You lived what time was left,
Brave and waiting for death,
Not knowing a Greater Love.

Peter Curry

CAT AND MUSE

I never gave thought to poetic form.
Terza rima and such, is not so much Dutch, but
Found in the language that Dante did clutch, where
Each rhyming sequence is named and is known, my
Lack of knowledge of such, makes me inwardly groan.
Many poetic masters, renowned for their essence of rhyme, are
Familiar with quatrains, saphics and stanzas,
I imaging they write them without second glances.
In all of these forms of classical meters,
I batter out lines as if with egg beaters, much
To the delight of my cat who just purrs, in
A rhythm I fancy that is classically hers.
She has an insight on a pen pusher's thought.
No dactylic measures has she ever sought, but
I'm working on things that will please her.
Instead of the games where I always tease her.
Perhaps a rondel or sonnet will do
Love may then blossom with skies ever blue.

If only
I could find the right buttons to press,
To learn classic forms, so I can impress
My cat who just purrs in a classical way,
Uniquely hers, I feel I must say.
I'm sure love would be mine forever the day, for
She, has lines classic, I feel I must say.

Richard Cluroe

HOMELESS

If life is full of swings and roundabouts
then why do I sit here motionless.
If life is full of swings and roundabouts
then why do I sit here motionless.
And should life be a bundle of laughs
why do I cry?
If home is where the heart is,
then I must be heartless, for I have none.
What a strange diet I keep
for less I eat each day
and record my weight loss by fading away.
If sleep is a cure for tiredness
then exhausted I must have been.
This shop doorway,
with begging hands outstretched
penniless shoppers I've seen.
With the same words uttered; to ears mostly deaf
muffled to those who seem not to care
the pedestrians, who stumble on death.
Then as they focus on their oasis,
while words evaporate in their steps
muted to my despair and call
'Any spare change? God bless'.

Andrew Sommerville Brock

THE MOVE

What a lot of work's involved
When you're moving house
Don't upset the neighbours
Be quiet as a mouse
Packing all the boxes
Emptying the drawers
Sweep the floor of the garden shed
And clean all the doors

Mother has been driving me mad
Packing up my room
She's gone and packed all my toys
I think it's much too soon
We haven't got a date to move
As far as I'm aware
She's packed up all my sister's dolls
And even her favourite chair

Daddy works away all week
Doesn't know what's going on
When he comes home weekends
He just sees what she has done
Just hope we can get moving
In the next few weeks
She's disconnected the dishwasher
Now we've had several leaks

The television is still working
But the video's packed away
She's packed all the CDs
So we've got nothing to play
She has also disconnected
Our link with Sky TV
Wonder how she'll watch her soaps
We'll have to wait and see

My sister is just as fed up
With what's going on
She has packed her bag also
And gone on the run
Think she's gone to Grandma's
Who will know what to do
If Mother keeps this packing up
Then I'm going too

At last the time arrives
And we'll be on our way
Goodbye to all our friends
Hurrah! It's moving day
When settled in our new home
One thing's for sure
I'm not moving anywhere
I'll be glued to the floor.

Martha Ann D'Souza

THE NEW HEADMISTRESS

She thinks she's very clever
Although she's half my age
She's proud of her endeavours
Her name's on every page
Outings, trips and projects
Who do they think they are?
While I'm stuck here with class five
Planning the bazaar
She thinks she's so original
The new ones always do
She's trained down under with Aboriginals
And plays the didgeridoo
She's rearranged her office
To get the best Feng-Shui
I wish the Head all the best
But hope she does not stay
She speaks about the pupil's needs
Free spirit and all that tot
She wears ankle chains and power beads
And thinks she knows the lot
The pupils think she's wonderful
They follow her around the school
They call me Mrs Misery
Because I quote the rules
They drift into my classroom
And proudly shout 'G'day'
I bite my tongue and grind my teeth
I hope she does not stay.

L Doel

WIND

Wind is a deadly thing,
Oh, I don't mean the weather kind
I mean the one down below.
You could be anywhere,
In a shop, there's nowhere to go
And all of a sudden,
There it goes without warning,
There it blows.
You can't escape it,
You can't hide
From that dreadful thing
Known as wind.

Marie Edwards

The Atmosphere Flyer

The night flying plane glides on
    Between two different levels.

The first level the clouds,
    The second one is ongoing
Ticking but without motion.

The atmosphere flyer, the never-ending clock.

He alone knows all the secrets, secrets lost
    At the dawn of time, and at the edge of eternity
Where pain through the draining of life
    Has made its home.

He flies from eternity to our reality
    To reap the harvest of the unfaithful multitude.

The plane still glides on through the night
    The first landing on earth and meeting
With mortals is one of sheer politeness
    Until the cunning of the fox takes over.

Please show us your eyes oh dark one
    You haunt my body through the night
Are we not your servants from the last millennium
    The atmosphere flyer the ultimate teacher
In extreme paranoia, zarathustras respected teacher
    And mentor.

        Never take pity on self-pity.

Alexander Eley

OFFICE GOSSIP

The truth is unwanted,
Believe what you will,
Perceive it your way,
Tell it with skill.
Make up the facts,
The story sounds good,
Hurt those involved,
Try to draw blood.
Lies are important,
Venom and spite,
Malicious, vindictive,
Personal as you like.
As long as you're happy,
With the damage you do,
Not a care in the world,
I'm glad I'm not you.

Colin Grimley

PARADISE

In paradise I hope there'll be
Time to drink my morning tea,
And savour it.
No need to rush,
Or join the jostle and the push
Of crowds on board the morning train.
No need to stand in fog again.
Or drip
In drizzle and in sleet
As I come home on tired feet.

In paradise I hope there'll be
A garden there, for you and me,
Where we can sit
And see the flowers.
Watch them bloom for hours and hours,
And never have to mind the clock
Or worry, as its tick and tock
Marks time
That rushes by so fast.
Is here and then, too soon, is past.

In paradise I hope I hear
Bird song always sweet and clear
Throughout the day.
Oh, what bliss!
So far away from all of this;
The noise, the bustle and the din.
'Twould seem a shame to let that in.
For in paradise
The sounds we hear
Should fall melodious on the ear.

In paradise I hope to be
With friends I love, and who love me.
Friendship is good,
Friendship is dear;
It soothes our woe and calms our fear.
So I hope there'll be good friends around
When at last I hear the trumpet sound.
Especially
The one friend true
Who has watched o'er me my whole life through.

Frances Marie Cecelia Harvey

LIMBO TANKS

They don't want to help people like us
Thousands screaming in stillness and crowded minds
Despair, a welcome reprise
Too pure a place for such a vacuum

Locked in the limbo tanks
Drugged like an animal for my own safety
Only we go nowhere but inside
Into another, still, lifeless room

With other neatly stacked humans
In pyjamas and iconic-like toys
Teddy bears like candy for company
Child-like screams, mad people's noise

Mummies come to visit
So classically British
Ignorance seeps from every orifice
She peels the patient's fruit.

Jo Hayton

OASIS

Living in hell
Dark storms surround me,
Almost blotting out the faint glimmer of
An oasis.

A reaching towards that light -
Then grasping fingers of fear dragging me back
To a constant stream of mixed emotions,
Strength ebbing away
As I wade through the debris
Of a dead past
And a dying present.

Mind and heart tinged with love and hate -
Bitter-sweet.
The feelings falling all around me
Threatening to squeeze and suffocate.

Light obscured in this hell-hole.
The knowledge of impending heartache.
Then panic gripping -
A pulling back of reins.
Only a faint glimmer of the oasis to cling to,
The brief smell of clean air
Keeping me afloat
In these black waters.

But the need to keep wading
Towards the light is strong
A craving for clean air to breathe -
Clean water to drink from my oasis -
My future -
With you.

Carol Hammond

LIVING FANTASY

On an undulating moor, a figure on a beautiful grey horse.
Armour in shining silver, with a golden lion on the crest of his brow.
'Know yourself, be yourself and the truth shall set you free.'
These words radiate from the big, proud warrior.
In the distance, a copse of birch trees wither and die.
The voice louder and more determined shouts,
'Know yourself, be yourself and the truth shall set you free.'
The moor dies faster, and faster,
withering and wasting quicker then the eye can see.
The beautiful horse, now transforms into an empty black husk.
Armour once shining, becomes tarnished.
A rasping, whisper, echoes from the corroded, rusted helmet.
'The truth is a lie, to be honest means your words are twisted.'
The lion pulses, for it was the one who spoke before.
It bellows its defiance,
'Know yourself, be yourself and the truth shall set you free,'
but the moor long dead and gone, none to hear its words.

Mark Henderson

THE DEMON DRINK

The monster's arrived!
With fiery tendrils
and talons of steel.
Piercing my mind,
with lies that kill.

The love he's promised,
the pain he's healed.
Yielding with delusion,
his watery shield.

The darkness hides
in his crystal eyes,
enshrouding my soul,
with invisible ties.

His voice, like silk
cuts at my heart.
Caressing my veins,
he slowly departs.

Till I'm kneeling in praise
of his casual gaze.
His world so pure,
'neath the hatred of life.

In slime so deep,
I drown as I sleep,
in a whirlpool of lies.

Debbie James

THE CANDLE OF THE HOLOCAUST
(For Eneicia Gia Bell)

I open the manuscript and begin to tell this story,
I will leave it up to you to judge, as you become the jury,
There's a flame of obscure darkness that burns for eternity,
For people that were so different joined in a forced fraternity,
Ignited by its pity this flame it burns so bright,
Inciting sorrow and darkness everywhere there's light,
Placed upon an iron desk in solitary prison cell,
As an inmate of this war it witnessed all the hell,
Smelling the stench of death as the fires destroyed the dead,
Watching the insanity as it crept into everyone's head,
Listening to the silent tears and cries of desolation,
Understanding the torment of their forgotten nation,
Backdrop to the stripes of slaughter and homicidal execution,
Illuminating only to that fascist institution,
Those sufferers of genocide stand at the fence and look,
Flickering in the candlelight we disturbingly close our book.

Katy Bryson (17)

SUICIDE THE ONLY ANSWER?

Questions, questions, thoughts so strong,
I've lost my way of where I belong,
Each day I live, I despise to the hilt,
My life is disjointed, my world on a tilt.

I look in the mirror, I don't recognise the face,
Just an empty shell, standing back from life's pace,
The pain inside is black and consuming,
My path in life has become so confusing,
The simple things like smiling have gone,
My face is shallow, I have lost all my song.

My body so heavy and hard to maintain,
I'm guilty and poisoned all I want is my grave,
The voice in my head is my only friend,
I need to know, when my torture will end,
I used to be happy, I used to be glad,
Now all that I am is quiet and sad,
A black cloud has shrouded my dark, dismal soul,
I feel I have fallen to the bottom of an endless hole,
I gather my thoughts of the friends I once had,
Now they have gone and the memories turned bad,
There is only one door for me to walk through,
Pills, drugs and alcohol to me they are true,
The only escape from this prison of mine,
To the good things in life now I am blind,
Who will miss me when I am gone?
A handful of people asking, 'What went wrong?'

Penny Buswell

MY OWN TERMS

I do my crying on my own
So that you do not have to see,
So that I can hide.
I do my crying on my own,
I fear the reason
You might be right,
I am only a child after all.
On my own terms
I tuck damp hair behind my ear
And curl into a pillow,
Sobbing and hitching for breath,
Hitching for breath and sobbing.
I do my crying on my own
So that I can wipe away my tears
And seek you out
Without you ever having known
Of my tears.
At times, I wish
For fingertips to wipe away,
For arms to comfort,
For a soul with answers.
And as much as I may crave interruption,
I do not want it to come.
Closed doors have seen my tears -
I know they will again.
It is not for personal power over you
That I keep this silence,
Deserving, loving husband.
It is because crying on my own
Is the only way I know.

Debra Bolton

RESPONSIBILITY

She feels alone.
She feels her life is
One commitment too much.
Her partner - now blind,
His guide dog now epileptic.
Her mother a victim of stroke,
Her father, so fit and strong,
Now with a dicky heart.

Her sister escaped to the US
Four children and a husband.
Enough commitment there for her.
Unable to be here,
No blame, no gain.
Wish her well, she deserves
Some fun in the sun.
A life with dreams fulfilled

She still feels alone,
However now aware.
That she learns so much
From all these responsibilities.
She learns to give with patience,
The joy of appreciating health,
The joy of loving unconditionally.
She recognises her dream fulfilled.

Babs Birkwood

EXCESS

Christmas Eve in the boot of a car
Grandad gulps neat whiskey
Monkey impressions.

Cluster round the pool table,
Mind the cues and balanced pints.
Familiar faces, I'd forgotten.

New pyjamas round the fire
Classic family viewing
Bouts of laughter.

Compulsory beer at lunchtime,
Traipse arm in arm down the road
Shiny boots crunch on snow.

Bottles of wine, flash at some cars
Smile for the camera
Watch the tree.

He stole away, just for an hour
Left his other life
Said he'd gone visiting

The first real emotion of the day
She smiles, strokes his hand
He leaves, back to reality

More wine, Gran found the sambuka
Grandad downs straight vodka
Father Ted impressions

The lights go out, her entertaining done,
He lies in bed
And plans tomorrow's escape.

Amy Blackburn

UNKNOWN WARRIOR

Say goodbye to the stars,
The wind on your face,
Your eyes full of sadness
You have fallen from grace.

Your ashes are scattered,
Thrown to the four winds,
The sun is on fire,
The land is barren.

A myth in your own right,
But brave to other's insight,
Youth ripped from your skin,
A darker shade of pale,
A deeper shade of pain.

The field where you cease to be,
The life drained from your veins,
In the darkness, alone you fell,
Never forgotten,
Forever tormented.

S Gelsthorpe

OWL LULLABY

The woozy, woolly owl was sleepy

The woozy, woolly owl was sleepy
when the round, round golden moon was going to bed.

When the round, round golden moon was going to bed,
the woozy, woolly, sleepy owl
blinking his round, round golden eyes,
couched in his comfy cosy nest,
inside the old, old hollow tree . . .

and the round, round owlish moon
did go to bed, as it should be.

Sylvie Alexandre-Nelson

FOR THE POLICEMAN WHO WAS STABBED -

No right that wicked had for this butchery
To run a river of blood from his chest vein.

The filth and evil in brain was there
Does not mean his heart had to bleed.

Many died and others laid life
Everyone talks but no strict action for terrorism.

That's liberty! So killing goes on
Only dictatorship might bring some discipline.

Anon

O WEYMOUTH

Sandy, sweaty crabs singing in the sea, singing for their misery.
Weeping Weymouth sulking as it skulks around wishing it were dead.
The father of the castle, no one can pass here not even my son and he;
the legs of an ewok, has to say the password:
Daddy Sand Rascal.
Fat tourists, me too, swinging and swaying with lumpy gut garbage.
I see a meaty ball of boy buried in sand jam.
The bearded boyfriend of my bleeding friend has paddles off to
free those crabs. Live to dig a hole in you: Weymouth.

Jo Overfield

SPEAKING THE UNSPEAKABLE

Anger, fierce, powerful anger.
Ride it like a Surfer.
Emotion curled in power
Hold it.
For the murdered children.

Murder for pleasure, swift amusement,
Enjoyment.
Habit forming
Sick, sick.
Spreading like a plague
Springing like a tiger.
Swift as a panther.
Eyes ablaze.

Ancient forces lurking, waiting.
Now it's moment, now the time,
Evil, dancing like flame.
Licking the ground - unapproachable,
Safe in the heat, waiting to burn
Humanity humiliated.
A vulnerable child snatched.
Screams unheeded, pleas ignored.
Lonely painful death.
Another child crying out.
Another scene of misery and terror.

Where are we?
Silent, useless.
Darkness flaunting its supremacy
Feeding upon our inertia.
Face the enemy, fight, fight,
Be very, very angry.

Helena Pell

FUTILE AMBITION

Within us all
Lies the prospect
Of great accomplishment -
To alter, assist and shape
The face of human kind.
Salmon-like we leap
And struggle past
The obstacles.
So many flounder
In the torrent -
Washed away by
The raging of the waters -
In the end?
Just the memory remains.

J Phelan

JEMIMA

There have always been wars, the ways of plundering, piracy, infamy
Etched down the ages, but the year was '97 of the 18th century.
After the bloody revolutions, they sailed over here from France
Glories to claim to every Frenchman, to capture the English lands
Invasion on the cockled shores, land in thousands there and more
February, they came to conquer Britain, they landed at Fishguard.
   Summon the Fishguard Fencibles, Colonel Knox.
The French soldiers turned to rabble, more riotous than unified
Raided every farm they set upon, stole every last drop of wine
Colonel Knox was at the ball when he was told of our plight
The Fishguard Fencibles, he thought, outnumbered, indefensible
' . . . are no match for the French army.' He chose not to fight.
   Summon the Stackpole Yeomanry, Lord Cawdor.
They met inside the Hall, men and weapons armed for blood and war
Ready to repel the invaders, marched in troops for them next morn'
Fishguard, Lord Cawdor sent message out to the French camp; a lie
'My forces are growing . . . surrender now or you'll be wiped out.'
French Commander, American William Tate sent reply 'We surrender
on condition . . . the men you have already captured are set free.'
Lord Cawdor was bewildered, his men had taken no French prisoners
But he would meet at the harbour, and accept the French surrender
Tate was to insist there had been Red Coats of the British Army
Red coats captured 20 of his men, others fled, urging him give up
But as 20 men were led into view, it was pitchfork wielding women
Red cloaks, traditional Welsh dress, marching them down the harbour
They'd tried to attack the women, but been taken prisoner instead
Britain owed her isle to these women, who had defeated the French
And the leader of our courageous ladies, a large imposing woman
Saluted Lord Cawdor, grinned, though rarely recalled by any of us.
Remember the Pembroke Mum's Army, her name Jemima Nicholas.

Jaegia

BENDING THE TRUTH

My wife is having an affair
with Uri Geller
oh, she denies it of course
but the evidence is there
it's in our spoons and in our forks
the set we only got at Christmas

buckled and contorted they hang
from their criss-crossing gallows
on the marbled, kitchen worktop -
if I had Uri I'd string him up as well

'They don't make them like they used to'
is all that she can say - a likely story

and how can she explain this - she can't -
when I confronted her and told her
from now on I'd be watching
the time that she comes home
my watch -
the one I've had these 20 years
stopped working.

Liam O'Meara

BLUE SKIES

Blue skies hang in-between my nights,
As shapeless lakes of space in time they lie,
Lightly suspended but heavy with wait;
Beautiful and wasted without you.

Sam Rawlings

TRUE LOVE

Love without another secret desire,
wild passion within the sensual fire.
To have kindness without the blindness,
to have and to hold with sheer need,
without the written deed,
Such! Would be the chemistry,
without the embittered jealousy.
Always enjoying the long embrace as you trace,
the detailed lines on that special face.
To love with an open heart,
is love from the complete start!

Victor Shaw

SPLIT INFINITY

Tortured face in the night
'Though I've known you for years
I take fright at the sight
Of your bulging-eyed stare
And the blade in your hand
Snaking out for my chest,
But your sharp, spittled curse
Tears me wide,
Hurts me worse
Than that blade going in
And I'm suddenly aware that
My sight's growing dim.
As my mind flashes clear
I try hard to stand,
Try hard to understand
How I misunderstood
From that moment we met
What was bad
What was good
And how love becomes hate.
Now it's really too late.
My dreams fade to an end
Spoiled in blood.
Truth descends
And I'm shamed by the stains
On my legs as I fall
And I realise I
Never knew you at all.

David Peden

RICH PEOPLE

Rich people don't have dogs,
They have 'pedigrees'.

Don't have cars,
They have 'Multiple Passenger Vehicles'.

Don't have money worries,
They have 'financial challenges that can be managed
        with the right investment portfolio'.

Don't get sick,
They have 'compromised health'.

Don't have doctors,
They have 'medical professionals'.

Don't have friends,
Just people who owe them money.

Jane Roland

KING COMMUTE

(Duet for a data inputter and a data shadow)

Captive by information
>
He already wears the boots

Held at bullet points
>
Of other dead men

In the space
>Behind the screen

The more I realise
He builds, resizes
The less I can visualise the unseen
The less, the less, the less the unseen

And yet
And yet
Behind my tired eyes
Behind his tired eyes
The more I visualise
The more he visualises, the more
I can realise things to be
He can realise things to be

As I type
>*On the bus someone wonders while the*

Wet on the window
Wet on the window makes
Christmas
Christmas of the
Traffic lights
Traffic lights

How many commute these days?
How many come back?

Lorenzo Quanla

THE WORLD IS LIKE A CIRCUS

The world is like a circus,
We people are the fleas.
Performing acts in life,
To please, or not to please.
Some are lions wild,
And need a lot of training.
Gentle are the dolphins,
Just want a little taming.
But like the trapeze artist,
Some of us fly too high.
Reaching out for things in life,
That somehow passed us by.
A few are like the chimpanzees,
And strike us very funny.
Then there are the high wire acts,
Who risk their lives for money.
Good troupes are the clowns,
Who make all others laugh!
Unlike the slithering snake,
A spiteful tongue to cast.
Some are like fine horses,
The thoroughbreds throughout.
Feel and kept well groomed,
And never to be without.
The circus has its ringmaster,
Over others to take charge.
Shouting out authority,
And crack the whip at large.
It takes all kinds of people,
To fill this great big world.
Compared to a circus, may sound a bit absurd,
Like animals in their cages, who perform perfectly.
In this world, like a circus,
All we want is to be free!

G Norman

WORLD TURNING

The world is turning
Round and round
And everyone listens for a different sound
Digging deeper
Struggling to survive
Ending up in the underground
To be creative
To make a beat
To put words on paper from the street
Hoping and wishing
Wishing and hoping
That tomorrow will be the day
When someone will say
You're going to be great one day!

Evelyn Stewart

THE PASSION

All men burn with a passionate flame,
Motivated by their fears and desires,
Some by their quest for fortune and fame,
Others by their need to show religious fervour,
But the wise man is consumed by the passion of love.

In love there can be no shadows,
No secrets concealed,
All must be shown and revealed,
With it comes the fear of rejection,
The earnest desire for acceptance.

Love lusts not for wealth or insubstantial things,
But for those though harshly tested, survive.
It accepts what logic cannot accept
Understands the most complex and meanings
Without knowing how or why.

It trusts, when there is no reason to trust,
Its faith is far greater than any known to man,
Faith, which is never blind but truthful,
Knowing all of a person,
Their darker and darkest sides
We still have faith in them.

It binds together dissimilar people
Of widely differing ages, races, religions and cultures,
You need never learn another language,
For the language of love is universally spoken.

It spans chasms that divide lovers,
The scoffers and doubters sneer at their naiveté
Until they see the 'impossible' made possible,
Until they feel that which they are most fearful of,
The passion of love.

Love is always humble, never proud,
Proud men are forced to admit, to their embarrassment and shame,
How wrong and foolish they are, yet feel
Strangely eased and peaceful by their self admission.

The man who allows love to flow is not perfect,
But by his admission of imperfections and flaws,
Through his willingness to try and change,
Knowing the heartache, troubles and quarrels that will arise,
Is as perfect as a human being as he can ever be.

Damien Plummer

THIS WONDERFUL WORLD

Have you stood at the foot of a mountain
In bright shining sunlight
And looked up to snow-covered peaks and ice fields
In this wonderful world of ours?

Have you gazed upon an age-old cathedral
Or a castle built high on a hill?
Have your thoughts turned in wonder
To a bygone man's labour and skill?

Or have you looked in sadness upon war-torn cities,
And wondered at man's inhumanity?

Have you seen the suffering inflicted
For the right to say 'this land belongs to me!'?

Have you seen a child wandering bewildered midst devastation
Or lying dead like a broken doll?
Have you seen a man, bereft of spirit, who cries
Or a woman wipe tears from her eyes,
Felt their fear and terror as man-made death falls from their skies,
As war-lords set nation against nation?

And if you have a god, have you prayed to him
That man will one day reach sanity,
And learn to share in peace and joy,
The beauty, the splendour of this wonderful world of ours?

Iris Robinson

UNTITLED

They sit there together
Like peas in a pod
Their minds are attuned
Like a well-strung guitar
The disapproval I feel
Is mine once again
The fire in the grate
Was it burning bright
Or was it the sound
Of my breaking heart?
Was it my want to be always alone
With this heartbreak of mine?
The cat's on the mat
The children are in bed
Cold is the wind in the world outside
But not as cold as I feel inside
For the want of my love
Who's gone far away
From these grey skies above
To a far better place than I'll never know
Was there no end to the pain?
Was there no release?
I'd come so close to my perfect dream
But now it had gone
Like a breath of wind
Never to return to this
Poor heart of mine

Patricia Turner

FIRE OF LIFE

Initially there seemed to be a spark
like lightning - ignited through the space
between us; jolting us as though a million volts
united us.
And from that first bright flame
there grew a conflagration that consumed
our hearts - our minds - and most of all, our bodies.
Devouring our reason. Blinding us to logic.
Oblivious to everything except that blazing fire
that for an age enveloped us.
But gradually the leaping flames were not so fierce.
The fire no longer all consuming; but rather
concentrated heat that permeated
every aspect of our being.
Hot glowing embers that only needed a passing draught
to stir them into instant life.
And so our unity continued. Comfortable, warm, serene.
Till karma reared its ugly head
and prematurely took away the tinder . . .
the reactor to my flint,
and the glowing embers faded into a mass of dying ashes
never to ignite again.
Never to produce that vital flame.
All sensation dead,
and only loving memories remain.

Ida Shewan

THERE'S A GREMLIN IN ME CUPBOARD

There's a gremlin in me cupboard
Only stands at two foot two
There's a gremlin in me cupboard
Drinking beer and sniffing glue
There's a gremlin in me cupboard
Says his name is Tony Blair
But the naughty little grizzler
Never combs his fuzzy hair
There's a gremlin in me cupboard
Always munching mice and flies
But he wanted some variety
So he's eaten all me pies
There's a gremlin in me cupboard
Singing songs and smashing plates
Now he's met a little monkey
And he's going out on dates
There's a gremlin in me cupboard
Says he came from outer space
There's a gremlin in me cupboard
You should see his ugly face
There's a gremlin in me cupboard
Or at least there was last night
When I went to look this morning
The scary beast was out of sight
There's no gremlin in me cupboard
I have no clue where he could be
But I never saw the monster
Since I gave up LSD

Joe Miller

001

I fear
No tooth or claw
No hand or paw

No foe on land or sea

No army that marches
In column and line

For the one thing
I fear is the end itself

The cloak and hooded one
That stalks all that walk
Upon this Earth

The death that walks

For we all shall see him

Just the once

And
When your hourglass has run out
You too shall feel the fear

And
Know you are the hunted

And
You too will realise there is no escape

So live well and full

For thee is nigh my friends.

Daniel O'Conner

SPIRIT

Don't break the spell
Don't take the spell away
In Hell, can't hear you yell
In Hell, you can hear and see
But you won't feel me
And I am lost in your soul
Dead in your heart
As doves when storm parts
When seas rage and
Foreboding strikes inside my fear
Like lightning, quick to race the air
Its target somewhere around
But here on the ground
Deep inside a stomach twirl
An aching cries
Calls to my heart
But what I treasure most
I won't part
As I know as mountains lie forever strong
My spirit tells of a spell of song
And of what calm to whom belong

Marc Ogilvie

APPLE CHILD

Sitting with the apples, the sunlight and the silver spiders
I could feel myself complete.
Up above the boathouse where the sunbeams fingered slatted shelves
And stretched out dreamily along the rows of ripening promise:
Yellow spilled with crimson, rich reds coursing over greens
A hoarded harvest waited, precious, safe.

No one came here in the afternoons,
Up the deep-lined treads of the rickety ladder
Into this sweet space. It was all my world.
I could hold the moment in a mouthful of warm juice
Roll back my tongue and draw the ripeness down
Sensing the illicit, squirreling my secret.

That hidden space was freedom for me then, unknowing child.
But now I wait to hear your step: you are my freedom now.

Maxine Relton

FADING

All this frustration
No inclination
Lazy, cul de sacs
Fit start elation
In dead occupation
Rutted in deep tracks

Where lies the answer
Among the cancer
Eating time away
Too old the chancer
St Vitus dancer
Sun setting on the day

Too much thinking
Between the drinking
Cooking up more dreams
Ambition sinking
Resented, stinking
Unpicked at the seams

Too young for dying
Too old for trying
Dusty old guitar
Between the crying
And whitish lying
Fading, shooting star

Matt Ward

ONE SUMMER'S DAY

Golden sun shines so brightly like the honey on the trees,
the grass looks like a carpet to walk over with the shadow
glistening over the morning dew.
Rabbits playing, and the birds singing.
The sun just rising while the mist by the river is appearing.
The birds flying, and the rabbits chasing each other and skipping.
The rabbits feeding themselves with the roots of the grass,
and nibbling at the ground.
The pigeons walking grand and looking for food,
and the blackbirds flying.
The morning is just about to be broken
with the pigeons flying onto the trees.
The sun shining with blue sky and white clouds that look like
you could sit on them.
The magpie is out looking for food while the baby rabbits
are playing together.
The sun is shining all around.
The fields look golden on the summer's day, so bright it shines.
The birds have just started singing.
The grey squirrel has just popped up to see what is going on,
and the magpie is still looking for food.
The blackbird is out as well, hoping bought with the cuckoo singing.
There are two squirrels jumping up the tree
looking for the acorns on the ground.
The rabbits making holes in the ground, nibbling at the grass.
The carpet looks like a golden haze from the sun
with the red heather shining.
The birds flying from tree to tree.
The magpie is still out plodding on.

Lindsey Way

CARPE DIEM

You saw me hapless and vulnerable,
out of my depth,
but smiled with kind understanding
- made me acceptable.

Tall and louche,
yet somehow gauche in your glasses
and strange
pauses.
In the break, over coffee,
you rolled tobacco nervously
and I sensed a love of lost causes.

You shuffled hope from foot to foot
and willed me to the pub
(didn't you?)
But I didn't notice
until you were gone,
until I relived the day again.

(And now?)
And now I whisper your name,
its echo crescending in waves
that swell to the rhythm of moonbeams
I swear I saw dance in your eyes
(or my dreams?)
And I wonder will I ever find you again . . .

Wendy Adele Williams

IS THERE ANYONE THERE?

The way was dark.
The shadows were lengthening and making weird shapes on the road.
It was frightening.
I was travelling along this road because there was no other way.
I thought there was someone behind me.
'Hello, is there anyone there?' I said in a shaky voice, but there was
                                                        no answer,
Only the leaves rustling in the breeze.
I hurried a little faster, and then I turned my head, but I couldn't
                                                see anyone there.
Then I heard a quiet voice. It was only a whisper.
'Do not be afraid. I am always by your side.
Just stretch out your hand, and put it in mine.
Walk in my footsteps and I will lead the way.'
Suddenly I was no longer afraid because this voice gave me a feeling
                                of peace and the strength to carry on.

Elizabeth Rita Williams

GIRL

Five earth years old,
You are the silky fruit
Of patient evolution:
Product of countless aeons,
Yet unaware of time's whorl,
Which, having created you -
Waits to destroy.

Your eyelids -
Fragile as innocence,
Flutter over pools
Of baby-blue beginnings
Spangled with sparks of hope
That dimly light your labyrinth
Of incipient, fearful life.

Dream while you can:
There is no Ariadne's thread
To lead you home:
Sad will be the day
When those eyes open
In a wrinkled face,
And see only a shroud.

Dave Austin

MY LADY

Where are you my dear?
In all this world where do you tread?
For I would know you from a silvery ghost
From and through the arrows in my chest.

Your eyes would make flight of my soul
Then I would know you, the one
The one that I would die beside
When my frame is to be no more youth.

Where are you my lady?
What sea must I travel to kiss your palm?
What chart must I pull from God?
Hide no more from me, throw your arms in the air and call for me.

I know not the language that you speak
Nor where your destiny lies
Or even for that matter the things stored in uncoloured eyes
But; my lady, what I do know, is that you are out there my love
And that my life will always be unreached till I hold your soul.

Gavin Joseph

LONDON'S WATERCOLOUR AIR

Watercolour Autumn sky and park,
The gallery at Dulwich watercolour outside and within;
The genius of a Turner is still needed here
To immortalise the softness of the scene in broad wash light and dark,
The russet maple leaf, the curving climbing road
Where trees, mature in confidence,
March past the chapel to the College of God's Gift
Where once I walked the day I was confirmed.

How could I know that forty-six years on
A mellowed and contented couple here
Would stroll and share the beauty of the day
Again in London's watercolour air
From vivid tropic sun in Singapore
And Persia's desert mountains clear and sharp?

Christopher Payne

HAPPINESS

Happiness is,
    A child's laugh,
    A bird's song,
    A flower's scent,
Happiness is,
    A priceless gift.

Happiness is,
    Present now,
    Not next week,
    Not 'in the future',
    Not 'to be worked for',
Happiness is
    Here right now.

Happiness is,
    A state of mind,
    Within us all,
    Not 'out there',
    Our inside light,
Happiness is,
    Inside us all.

Happiness is,
    Loving and giving,
    Self-acceptance,
    God's world around us,
    But most of all
Happiness is,
    Love.

Happiness is,
Within our grasp,
Just stand back,
Take time for yourself
And you will find
Happiness is
Yours right now.

K M Oyediran

UNTITLED

No hiding place
From this statue of grace
Time suspended
Dancing jewels
And cool clear crystals
Ease into your mind
Earth discovery
Spins a golden thread
I tremble at the fall
Entertain thoughts
Like guests leaving
Wondering about the dream

Michael Phillips

SPIRIT DANCING

Undulating effortlessly
Clutching at spirits following me
My shape is shifting constantly
Unbound and floating free.

Embed Pbrush

And every frame I try to freeze
Unfreezes, like a rippling pool
Like shadows, phantoms in the dark
My reach, un-reaching finds no mark.

My fingers flirt with empty air
While dancing on without a care
My body learns to sing its part
In a soulful symphony to my heart

My feet don't fall on earthly ground
I let the spirits spin me round
Submitting to a sensual flow
Nam-myoho-renge-kyo

Kath Posner

THE LAST DANCE

Spin around; touch the ground, my precious little jewel,
You clearly stole my heart away, how could you be so cruel.
I was thunderstruck, mesmerised, and captured by your spell,
Seems love had sadly blinded me, you cold-hearted Jezebel.
You're a user, an abuser, a wicked siren oh so sly,
A temptress with those dancing feet, until you'd bled me dry.
Spin around; touch the ground, my precious little jewel,
Another victim's passed your way, how could you be so cruel.
You've cheated, mistreated, one more turning of the screw,
I've watched you from afar too long; my heart is torn in two.
You've danced your last dance little swan, with a curtain call I see,
How many more hearts to be broken, how many other fools like me?
My hand was clearly shaking; my mind had taken flight,
The ovation was deafening, as I escaped like a thief in the night.
They say it was a mystery, a wayward spirit's lucky chance,
A thousand eyes were upon you, as you danced your greatest dance.
Oh, you looked so beautiful, with elegance and grace,
But now the little swan's no more, she's gone without a trace.
Spin around; touch the ground, my precious little jewel,
Revenge is sweet my pretty one, how could I be so cruel.

Jan Yule

COUSIN

We were together for an afternoon.
We walked through fine gardens,
Beneath trees that waved above our level heads,
Into dark chapels, gazed at unwieldy Lazarus
And surnames chiselled out by two World Wars.
She was well and laughed and seemed quite undisturbed.
We talked about things which meant so much to us
But which now served only to hide a disappointment
Such as children feel for their parents when they find
That a school term's left them amiably unchanged.
Before she left our words flew to and fro,
Ethics, passions, principles, intents,
Drowning our kinship's quiet eloquence.

Jeremy York

CHARISMA

Just the names,
Kobe Bryant,
Vlady Divac,
The sheer spelling,
Captivates one's mind,
Like the pure aerial manoeuvres,
Gliding through the hot stuffy air of the arena,
Finishing with a tremendous 'thud',
As the bad falls,
Helplessly through the basket.

Defenders stand,
Eyes fixed on the flying player,
As he cuts the air with his body.
The basket,
Situated ten feet off the ground,
Eagerly collects the ball,
Not only affected by gravity,
But by the sheer pressure,
Of the seven foot player,
As he drives it through.

Daniel C Wright

TOP OF THE STAIRS

Peaceful,
Quiet,
Those are just two of the words
That come to mind.

Work here,
Work there,
Work on table,
Work on chair,
Work everywhere.

Then suddenly the golden silence
Is shattered by the kids
Going out to play.

Pounding on doors,
Shouting at each other,
Bouncing balls in corridors,
Banging on windows.

Sometimes it's cold,
And I can feel the icy wind
Circling my ankles,
Sending shivers through my body,
Making me feel almost paralysed,
But in spite of all that,
I'm quite content
Sitting at the top of the stairs.

Pauline Reynolds

ENLIGHTENED

You're very open, explore the world
You're conscious, but ignore the gossip
You enjoy every minute of what's your life
There's always something in it if you look inside
You consume information, take what's rightfully yours
You encourage light, listen and then respond
I'm enlightened by this very intimate bond
Your eyes are opened wide
My questions are answered sooner
Our understanding is greater than demanding
You know of life's pleasures
You show me you'd go to any measures
To make the most of what is yours
Before you're a ghost behind closed doors
You've enlightened me with your wide scope
I'm attached to an invisible safety rope
I'm never frightened, always enlightened.

Paul Ross

CONFLICT

Guns - war - atrocity
Blood - death - futility

Linda Roussel

THE SONG OF THE FOREST KING

The sacred groves are gone, the mistletoe has died; no voices are
singing the ancient song of the king and his woodland bride:

'When all the grass was green
And all the birds did sing,
How beautiful were the white rowan trees
In the woods of the forest king!

The honey and the wine,
Red roses by the bower,
A year to be loved, then a day to die,
So we cherish each golden hour.

Our lamp of love burns bright,
It binds and blinds our eyes
To all but the spell of the timeless trees
And the beasts of our paradise.

Then winter nights return,
Orion strides the sky
And soon are the saplings in bud again
To remind us that soon we'll die.

The hunters stalk the woods,
Their raucous shouts ring clear:
'And who is to murder the king today
And be lord of the trees for a year?'

The terror and the pain,
The blood that stains the grass
Are the only tokens of all the love
That will die with me now, my lass.

When all the grass was green
And all the birds did sing,
How beautiful were the red rowan trees
In the woods of the forest king!'

Archie Buchanan

A Spent Cartridge

Ryan lay looking at the stars
When the mist lifted. Only
Restricted by the Velux window,
Its frame as bars to the trees,
To the houses round about,
To all outside energy interrupting.

He can watch the stars
And even see the moon
When the clouds withdraw
And the curtains part
On the view of many heavens.
Patterns, lights like a runway
To lift off, escaping into space,
Free! There, he could move anywhere
Except for the soles of his feet
Or the inert indent of his form
On the mattress in his room.

Yet he could beat gravity
And storm a way through space,
So that soon his weight
Was irrelevant, or so it seemed.
A case of a spent cartridge.

Diane Burrow

THEATRE OF DREAMS

Where dreams come true
The day is just perfect
You are with the people you love
Your happiness is complete

The life you live
Is your life and no one else's
You make your decisions
You have total control

Life is very complicated
You never know what will happen next
Today your life is good
Tomorrow serenity

There are always bad days
Good days we always welcome
They hide the hurt and fears
Happiness is closer than you think

Relax, today is for living
Live in the theatre of dreams
Your life is just beginning
There is sunshine in every day

Live for now.

Carole A Cleverdon

ADVICE ON LIVING

Don't rock the boat
Don't make any waves.

Keep a low profile
Then you'll be safe.

Don't make a stand
You'll be left out on a limb.

Don't push yourself forward
You'll be shot down in flames.

Don't say this
And don't say that.

Don't fall in love
He'll break your heart.

Don't grieve your elders
Just be polite.

Just keep on smiling
Don't look forlorn.

Just pardon me - for being born!

Opal Innsbruk

NOT AN ORDINARY DAY

Not an ordinary woman.
I've learned you are a beautiful woman but I have to leave you.
There are enlightened beings who live only to help other people.
Black is a beautiful colour until death comes.
A thinner jumper for Mum and think when you are doing things.
I remember all those women before you and none after.
Time goes quicker when you smoke.
I won the race but lost the girl.
A heart and lungs didn't do Leroy much good.
It's not an ordinary day and you are not an ordinary woman.
The only thing to say is goodbye.

Alan Cornelius

THE OLD ONES

They're placed like sentinels around the room,
respectful distances apart.
But inert, turned blindly towards a screen, a rage of colour
and noise which falls upon deaf ears.
They nod, they loll, they stare, unsmiling, uncomprehending.
But inside one of them cries, 'Hello dear! You've brought a drop
of sun with you today.
Your mum's been good. Ate up all her dinner.'
And Mother, vaguely aware, head half-turned, presses 'play'
from fifty years ago, and sees a little girl run with open arms
and swings her up and asks, 'How was school today?' and
'Did you eat your greens?' and 'Who put your plaits in the inkwell?'
Another sees her handsome man, in uniform, swinging along,
a splitting grin, and feels again that long forgotten thrill.
He's waiting somewhere, Lord - a silent plea - take me home,
Yet another, munching long since with his mates in some
works canteen with 'Workers' Playtime' blaring out,
thinks that he might have a pint tonight. Betty won't mind,
the kids'll be in bed, and there'll be something on the wireless.
Betty's always been the one. She'll be here soon.
The strangers who crowd his daylight hours are hiding her away.
Every day he smiles and nods towards the door.
There is no other face he knows. His wait is endless. Heigh-ho!
And while I stand and watch and smile
I catch these echoes from minds still clear with pictures.
I stoop and kiss a papery cheek.
My mother's eyes look up.
She tucks the plaits behind my ears.
I am her little girl.

Jan Crocker

GLADE

I wish your skin
Were such fine petals
So I could press them
Then learn to treasure things.

Like your dance you dance
And the songs you sing
Songs that only make sense
To you and no one else.

And your dreams became fragments
Commencing of my little life
And so will fall the autumns
Gliding down upon your smile.

But now, I dance your dance
And I sing your songs
And they always make sense
For you are my life
And nothing else.

Emma Bone

THE COLD STONE

What terminal do I come?
A terminal just a stopping place
A pick up stop
Waiting the lonely heart
In its isolation
Of ever increasing beats.

We feel a tendency
Of circumstance
Some operation -
We question and feed that fire,
We except the ritual
We turn and ask for answers
We find one star above
The paper of our obituary
And the silent voice
In the darkness of night
Without a colour or code
Just the initials on the cold stone.

Roger Thornton

HIGH ANXIETY

Fighting with fear - I float beside myself
At war with thoughts that need a shelf
Hugging and rocking to keep sanity
Restraining the child who wants to be free.

Christine Nicholson

ALL ALONG THE LINE

Axis of evil,
world in the balance,
holding up well

A mind to kill
over matters of chance,
axis of evil

Proven skill,
Lords of the Dance
holding up well

A native appeal
at first glance,
axis of evil

Drawn to still
a sure advance,
axis of evil
holding up well

R N Taber

THE UNWRITTEN WORDS

I view my world
Through starry skies at night
Valleys green in many shades of light
The trees that murmur
In the whispering breeze
And the wandering waves
That roam the seven seas
The wild dog rose that rambles up the hill
The drifting feather
Or a torn-out quill
I view my world
Through life's unwritten words
The music of our many calling birds
From mountain peaks
To oceans deep and wide
The sun and moon, master of the tides
I view my world in wonder as I stroll
From her painted skies
To the fire in her soul
But this world is just a home
For you and I
We must treat it with respect
As we pass on by

Brian Wardle

No Emergency

A fire engine siren sounds in the distance
it nears closer with each passing second
I don't know why. There's no emergency here
our fires abated years before.

An old Bowie song plays upon the radio
reminds that I once possessed passion
when life was full of hate and love
now it just serves up cold indifference.

Bacon and sausages sizzle in the pan
like something exciting should happen;
but the suitcase left with you last night;
I liked that suitcase.

Jeff Brooks

PHOTOGRAPHIC MEMORY

Being stared at by this procession of
Paralysed creatures attempting to
Assume a posture for posterity
Appeals to me not at all.
Standing as if bolted in that absurd
Silence
That became a
Silver oxide complacency of album smiles,
They fixed me in obsolescence -
Quickened before the shutter shut.

Flagstones of grey cardboard -
Flakes of rectangular time,
Split and dog-eared,
Fold past my reluctant thumb
To conceal the eager, innocent selves
That we once were.

Reaching a certain snap,
A time delay chaffs against the impulse
To supply the sound-effects: the slash of
Red-painted spade into wet sand,
The whirry of windmill blades
Abandoned after so much pleading.

Landscapes lead away from eye,
Lax-angled by the cunning composer,
Tidier of tree lines,
Smoother of verges and ditches.
A road caught moving off
Into the escaping
Horizon
Is a pictorial map,
Pocketed after so much re-routing.

Confronting the insinuating background
Encrusting the subject -
Whether 50's motor car,
Shingle beach,
Or model aeroplane held aloft -
I recognise this view of incongruity,
The past.
Recorded not by me,
But by the omniscient,
Self-regarding camera.

Robert Kennedy

FATHER TO SON

What makes this hurt haunt me?
I find no solace in silence
How can care be still, cool, composed?
His indifference isolates,
Anger flames in fury at powerless parenthood.

A child in tears tears at my heart
Memory of vulnerable child warmly
Rescued in the deluge hugs my heart.
But now it is as distant as a time trap,
The iron-toothed bar slammed shut
We could share, even now,
If only we might return to innocence.
But criticism cramps my heart,
And he flings his 'freedom' in my face.

Martin Dore

DE PROFUNDIS

Callous, cold, contorted clouds
Of conniving gloom hover hysterically
Over a hideous, hueless horizon, haunting
Our weary world with wretched woes!
In the crimson conflagration of terror,
Torment, torture, wanton destruction
And death, the yawning, black abyss
Of despair opens upon stunted, segregated
Dreams, hapless expectations, in the sinuous,
Murky, constricted cracks of squalid humanity!
We hear cocked, loaded guns booming furiously,
From east to west and from north to south,
On the smouldering dunghill of dismal,
Desecrated desires locked in the tantalising
Reality of disillusioned innocence lost in
The horrendous whims of lingering tragedies!
Warped images of tainted purity, beguiled
And betrayed, billow, as sullen, calculating
Children caper with crimpled conscience
And castrated future in the caustic cauldron
Of colossal carnage! But a faint, tiny voice from
Deep within the bruised brotherhood of mankind,
Whispers wholesome words of love and peace,
Even as the feeble, frail, forsaken flame of faith
Flickers feverishly in our very darkest hour!

Keith Simmonds

DRIFT

Birds flew overhead.
Warm air whispered to my face
I paused and thought . . .
. . . as I watched more and more,
time had no existence as now the sun was setting,
clouds seemed to say nothing but glisten
forming a haze that assisted the red, glowing sun.
Each shape in the sky had a difference,
redone with the twilight and the silhouetted glow.
The waves comforted my sense while
being sprayed as each one crashed from each rock.
Sand dunes added more feel,
with every step grains of sand flowed
through gaps between toes and made me remember;

I exist.

Ali Taft

UNTITLED

Are you a victim
to your
own emotions?
Do they stop
all the commotions?
Do you wish
that you
were stronger?
And hold out
for very much
longer?

P Allen

ANGER

Low and deep,
A flickering flame,
Simmering in your soul.
Waiting, waiting.

A little spark,
It starts to boil,
In the pit of your stomach.
Rising, rising.

Prickly heat,
Heart racing fast,
Trembling from head to toe.
Souring, souring.

Aaaghhh
Bang!
Wooshhhh.
Falling, falling.

Sarah Bray

CAN YOU ... ?

Can you taste me, can you hear me
When we are apart?
Can you sense me, can you feel me
Inside of your heart?

Can you feel me clawing at the edges?
Squeezing out your blood?
The way I always wanted to
The way I never could.
Do you feel me when you're all alone
When there's nobody else there?
Get used to being alone,
Because people just don't care.

Can you see the hate in my eyes
Every time you look at me?
I hope it sends shivers down your spine
The way that it should be.
Do you taste my blood as I lick my wounds
Which you made appear?
For all this pain that you have caused
You've got much more to fear.

Chloe Lees

DESTINY

As free bloweth
'tis wind ye sing,
sad thy moon,
cold dark night soon,
ye heart that beats,
thunderstorm that reaps.

'Tis ship that sails,
hi cometh hi tide,
'tis call wee fowl,
lost in paradise,
sad paranormal eyes.

Too many 'tis day,
many fall low,
tragic thump by all,
upon thy tree stump,
forego ye poor soul.

Heartbeats drum,
mind brazen prison doom,
upon bleak moor,
lost in thy mist,
strand'd soul twist'd
upon thy broken bow.

Devil's thro' haunt'd
ye poor wretch'd soul,
not thy be tomorrow,
wot heart thy see,
destiny tearful be,
languidly await thee.

Wlodzimier Kajon

MIND THRASHING

Outrage and anger,
deep-seated passion.
Contorting internally,
without rhyme or ration.
Emotions like storm,
erupting and clashing.
Leaving transfixed,
like eternally smashing.
Always frustrated,
- always mind thrashing.

Gary J Finlay

THE BALLOON

Still it clings there,
Caught on the holly tree,
Wrinkled like an ancient face,
Bedecked with ribbon's curls,
Remnant of party's joy,
Of smiles and fun
And sticky hold; tight
But not quite enough.

Still it clings there,
Hanging on for very life,
Buffeted by wind and rain.
How like me it is to see,
That yellow balloon,
Child-like in tenacity,
We will not let go
For fear of the end.

Karen Hillman

UNTITLED

Restore the years
That the locust
Has eaten in his life.
I know you've used
The pain and struggle
But I'm crying
Out for him
Yet again.
Surely it must be time -
Time for wholeness,
Time to
Restore the years
That the locust
Has eaten in his life.

Natalie Jagger

VERDICT

Polished pillars rose before
The butchered oak
From where He spoke

'You can be absolutely convinced
That you are absolutely right
And be absolutely wrong'

The faithful stood silent
Murmuring splinters
Barely disturbed
Each stone
Clustered
Alone

Convinced?
Absolutely?

Each stone smiles
Clean crisp creases,
Increasing year by year,
With guiding tongue
And glassy eye
Insisting: 'Right - or - wrong?'

Piercing splinters fell before
The butchered oak
From where He spoke:

Right - or - wrong?
It shocks, shatters, cracks
Each pillar, each
Congregated stone

Marble eyes see nothing.
And about that I am

Convinced. Absolutely.

C Holmes

THE LITTLE GIRL

A little girl was asleep in the corner of the street,
Her clothes looked cheap and there was nothing on her feet.
Through malnourished and animal-like her beauty still shone,
And held tight to her chest a headless doll.
As I sat and wept, my coat acting as her cover,
My eyes I did close, whispered one prayer after another,
After I walked away crying, after all that could be done,
I turned for one last look but she was gone.

Cassius James

THE VELVETS, THE STOOGES, THE PISTOLS AND YOU

Feeling cold, frustrated and angry
gimme something to hold
the Velvets, the Stooges, the Pistols and you
the sun is shining on a warm spring morning
everyone you see is smiling until they see you
why can't you smile as well?
Instead you feel that only the worst is due
the Velvets, the Stooges, the Pistols and you
black t-shirts, old Levis,
black shoes, tired hair and resigned face
the Velvets, the Stooges, the Pistols and you
I had it all
owned all the best music, took all the best drugs
smoked for broke, drank an ocean
died at least twice
woke up in bed next to strangers
cried at night and slept where I fell
always a state of haste and hate
anger and hurt, on my own
but I always had
the Velvets, the Stooges, the Pistols and you.
You, who I could touch and feel the breath of against my face
when the most desperate hour came and hung over me
and get an answer from a question
the Velvets gave me an answer
the Stooges gave me an answer
the Pistols answered
but most of all there is you who I can touch and feel
the Velvets, the Stooges, the Pistols and you.

Jack Karney

THE ROSE

At the heart of the garden
A rose
Golden and glowing.

Leaves richly dark
Buds
Fatly growing.

Protective and loving
The bloom's secret spines
Abrasively stating
'This beauty is mine!'

Vera Morrill

WORKING LIVES

Startled from sleep within their heads
Synthetic chimes echo, they leave their beds
Unmade today as those before
Another futile household chore
Abandoned in flight to desk and chair
The breeding mounds of paper there
Herald a day longer than the night just past
'Morning', 'Morning', hollow greetings cast
By those who 'would leave yesterday'
But for the sop of monthly pay
Each enamoured by unrealised dreams
Retirement cottages, pension schemes
Seem father off each monotonous hour
Even youthful ambitions rapidly sour
Under the pressure and the criticism
The caffeine-fulled somnambulism
That scar for most each working day
Lives mortgaged to a cabaret
Frustrated by bureaucracy
Deprived of equanimity
Few have strength to break their thrall
Some feign indifference to freedom's call
Escape is then so easily found
In a narcotic haze or a tumulus mound

Julian F Murfitt

OFFICE RITUALS

Circling, like cranes, and stood off into smiles
while, fish-eyed and starey, action follows work
he is caught up on the corridor
snapshot to a dance in a space both share.

Considered; considerate - those attributes again
as, elaborate and gestural, costumed manoeuvres
set-piece interest or, glassed within cages,
procrastinate meaning to balance what he says.

Agreements; and difference. Those finely-sewn
feathers, kite-lines, glitter and dressings
to make good - or hook and eye stirrings
when the bottom line drums and agreements unravel,
drawing up feeders from the pool.

Now, shivered by dissent, the pool-eye winks
as, bird-like, storkish, he side-steps to call time
angle, dreaming, to wing-stretch difference
and view a separate god - as if he felt the wind
of some lost world, keyholed towards life,
or, blindfold through the labyrinth,
talked wishes on the couch, flightless as the boy
with night light lifted, confiding all he missed.

Leslie Tate

NASTY PIECE OF WORK

A bully is a coward,
Who hasn't many friends,
He isn't really big or tough,
He only just pretends!
As long as someone's different,
In any shape or way,
He'll find the words to hurt you;
He'll find something to say!
As long as someone's smaller,
You know he'll have a 'go' -
But you *must* confide in someone;
Someone special who you know!
You can tell your mum and dad,
Or teacher or a friend.
Bullying is stupid,
And it has got to end!

Julie Taylor

HAPPINESS

Happiness is often a most elusive thing,
Not always found on mountain tops,
The little things that bring
Great joy to most of us, but fail to recognise
That we are holding in our grasp
A very special prize,
Sometimes only fleetingly
It tends to slip away
Leaving desolation,
A darkening of the day.

Those first wee steps a baby takes
Or long awaited word,
Happiness comes with them
Such pleasure they afford,
The whispered words 'I love you'
A tender, loving kiss,
Are memories to treasure,
Happiness is this.

Sunrise, sunsets, those visual sights
Blest enough to share
With someone very close to us,
Happiness is there

And later in reflection
When years have rolled away,
Taken loved ones with them
The skies above are grey
Remembrance is the golden key
Our lonely hours to bless.
Thinking of those many gifts
That brought us happiness.

Ellen Thompson

THE SUMMER HOUSE

May I avail myself of the tranquillity
That nestles here between your shapely beams
May I rest, just for a while,
In what cool shade your benches can afford
When the sun is high?
May I enjoy the sweet scent of the roses
While I gaze in wonder at the maze
Of blossoms in abundance that surround you
The diversity of colour, form and size.
I'll sit quite still and quiet, I promise,
While the birds flit to and fro;
I'll enjoy the gentle breeze
And allow the swaying of the trees
To calm my frantic thoughts,
To lull me to sleep perhaps,
At least, to peace of soul.
The grass is greener here
Save where I've trailed my weary feet
By seeking solace here so often
Amidst the hanging baskets and the climbing ivy
That distance me from the road nearby,
From the very noise of life
And make this valued haven, my retreat.

D J Totten

As You Watch Them

Laying horizontal at peace
Black sofa they lay
Praying like hand shapes
Deep in
Dreaming on
Cushions at the three, red in colour too

A rubbing of a nose
Twitching
Even snoring (real loud)
With a little talking to boot

I look right in front of me
Movies - TV - or even the BBC
But dreamer
Beautiful - appealing
Try it
Watch them sleep

E A Triggs

Out Of This World!

I stepped off my world
And entered your planet.
I saw shooting stars
And an eclipse.
In awe of your total presence
I made discoveries of my own.
Night turned to day,
Winter became spring,
Chaos found peace
And you released a poet!

Sue Umanski

MAYBE

We all can see our own reflection
in another's grief,
stopped by realisation that we hold
not even our own fate in our hands.
That pain we feel, stabbing away at our hearts
cannot explain the unknown fear that lurks like a shadow,
haunting us in our darkest hour.
To know we control not the reins, but freefall along life's path,
those who fall off the cliff's edge,
doomed it seems from the start,
yet we will get our day,
just like all the rest,
and life, it will keep hidden its secrets,
maybe it's best we don't know them.

E Uprichard

READING 'JAWS' AGED TEN

Chrissie swam in darkness:
I turned a page.
The great fish homed in
on sound waves.
She didn't stand a chance.

With a violent jolt
her leg was off, pulsing blood
fathoms down.
She frenzied
- luring him back
to the night-time feast.

He rammed her body
up from sea, gauged flesh
with razor-teeth.
Then . . .
the book snapped shut.

I was injured.

Barry Woods

LONESOME

Down the concrete road
Rolls a battered half pint
Can of tin, signalling

Its lonely din.

A speeding tyre
Ends its deadly jingle.
I mourn its lonesome signal,
Breeze grows to bluster,
Threatening more to muster.

G West

SUBMISSIONS INVITED
SOMETHING FOR EVERYONE

POETRY NOW 2003 - Any subject,
any style, any time.

WOMENSWORDS 2003 - Strictly women,
have your say the female way!

STRONGWORDS 2003 - Warning!
Opinionated and have strong views.
(Not for the faint-hearted)

All poems no longer than 30 lines.
Always welcome! No fee!
Cash Prizes to be won!

Mark your envelope (eg *Poetry Now) 2003*
Send to:
Forward Press Ltd
Remus House, Coltsfoot Drive,
Peterborough, PE2 9JX

**OVER £10,000 POETRY PRIZES
TO BE WON!**

Judging will take place in October 2003